S/HE
BRAIN

S/HE
BRAIN

SCIENCE, SEXUAL POLITICS, AND THE MYTHS OF FEMINISM

ROBERT L. NADEAU

Westport, Connecticut
London

Library of Congress Cataloging-in-Publication Data

Nadeau, Robert, 1944–
    S/he brain : science, sexual politics, and the myths of feminism /
Robert L. Nadeau.
        p.   cm.
    Includes bibliographical references and index.
    ISBN 0-275-95593-1 (alk. paper)
        1. Sex role.   2. Gender identity.   3. Sex differences (Psychology)
    4. Brain—Sex differences.   5. Feminist theory.   I. Title.
    HQ1075.N32   1996
    305.3—dc20   96-3211

British Library Cataloguing in Publication Data is available.

Library of Congress Catalog Card Number: 96-3211
ISBN: 0-275-95593-1

First published in 1996

Praeger Publishers, 88 Post Road West, Westport, CT 06881
An imprint of Greenwood Publishing Group, Inc.

Printed in the United States of America

The paper used in this book complies with the
Permanent Paper Standard issued by the National
Information Standards Organization (Z39.48–1984).

10 9 8 7 6 5 4 3 2 1

TO MY MOTHER, MARY NADEAU,
AND TO MY DAUGHTER, LANGDON NADEAU,

WITH MY FULL LOVE AND DEVOTION

Contents

CONTENTS

Preface

Those of us who attempt to assess the societal impacts of new scientific knowledge often feel like less than welcome guests in public debates for good reasons. We are often the bearers of disturbing news, and many of our dire predictions are not realized. The disturbing news is that science has disclosed differences in the brains of men and women that have behavioral consequences, and the dire prediction is that this knowledge will be abused in the service of sexist agendas.

With this prospect in mind, my first impulse in writing this book was to provide a reader-friendly account of what science actually says about the sex-specific human brain. The rationale was that if those of us concerned about issues of sexual equality were more familiar with this research, we would be better prepared to expose the sexist abuses and obviate their invidious influence. I eventually realized, however, that the greatest dangers as we assimilate this knowledge is not sexism per se. It is extra-scientific cultural variables that have nothing to do with sexism.

For the last thirty years, legal definitions of sexual equality in the United States have been predicated on the assumption that gender identity is learned in gender-neutral minds and that sex, or biological reality, is not a determinant of this identity. During this same period, this assumption also legitimated the sex/gender system in feminist theory and the vast educational enterprise built on this theory. The problem, simply put, is that the human brain is not sex, or gender, neutral. Since differences in the brains of men and women condition learning and cannot be obviated in the learning process, there is an undeniable connection between biological reality and gender identity.

When I first realized this was the case, I gave serious thought to abandoning this project. I am no stranger to controversy in academic debates in fairly esoteric areas, such as scientific epistemology, quantum cosmology, and cognitive science. Yet this debate could have very negative real-world consequences and involved social and political issues that were daunting in both scope and complexity.

The fact that I live in a university community where large numbers of faculty have built their academic careers on feminist theory was also a cause for concern. Since many of these people are in positions of authority, the decision to publish a book that challenges the integrity of this theory could adversely impact my career ambitions and opportunities. On the other hand, there are occasions when larger commitments dwarf personal liabilities, and this, I concluded, was clearly one of them.

If science had "merely" disclosed that the human brain, like the body, is sexed, enlightened philosophical and moral concerns should take precedence over this discovery. Nature, however, is almost invariably more subtle that common sense allows, and that is certainly the case here. What we know about the evolution of the sex-specific human brain and the manner in which the sex-specific differences must be understood can not only eliminate much of the confusion and conflict in the politics of our sexual lives. It can also lead to a quite remarkable and totally unanticipated result—a new standard for sexual equality that would eliminate the grossly unequal treatment of women sanctioned by the current standard. While these claims, I realize, are extraordinary, advances in scientific knowledge have often dispelled the ignorance that fuels our darker impulses. As I hope to demonstrate, this definitely applies to research on the sex-specific human brain.

In interdisciplinary studies of this kind, the list of those who should properly be thanked tends to be impressively long. There are, however, two people to whom I am particularly grateful, and the book is dedicated to them. To my mother, the hope is that other women will never endure another dark age of sexual inequality like that which she knew virtually all of her adult life. To my daughter, the hope is that the age in which she lives her adult life will witness the dawn of a global community in which men and women are co-equal actors on the stage of this troubled world. If this book represents a step, however small, in these directions, the decision to open what is likely to be a very acrimonious debate will not have been as foolish as I have sometimes imagined.

CHAPTER 1

The American Gender War: Sex, Gender, and the S/he Brain

If the sexes are at war, it is not a war that can be fought to the finish. We need each other too much for that.

—ELLIS COSE
A Man's World

The story that would capture the American psyche was about a sadly inadequate couple living in northern Virginia named John and Lorena Bobbitt. As everyone seems to know, the saga began when Lorena responded to her sexually violent husband with some violence of her own. She cut off his penis with a large kitchen knife and threw the severed organ into a parking lot. The penis was then recovered by the rescue squad, taken to a hospital where John had previously been admitted, and surgically reattached.

In the weeks that followed, John and Lorena became the subject of a fierce national debate that was rather neatly divided along gender lines. While most of the male commentators expressed sympathy for Lorena, they did not feel that her behavior was innocent. Even if the knife-wielding deed had been provoked by attempted rape, they could not justify this Freudian nightmare. But there was little support for this view from the female commentators. As most saw it, Lorena

Bobbitt was not only a heroine in the fight against male sexual aggression; she was also the emblem of all sexually abused women in a culture in which women are collectively dominated and controlled by men.

Kim Gandy, executive vice president of the National Organization of Women, sympathized with the many women "who have gone through this and probably wish they had a chance to get their revenge."[1] In *Vanity Fair*, Kim Masters reported on "Lorena supporters who have transformed the V-for-victory sign into a symbol of solidarity by making scissor-like motions with their fingers."[2] On my own university campus, the in-joke was that Lorena had recently been seen greeting John with this gesture and saying, "NOW do you get it?"

One of the more colorful commentaries on penis as symbol of male sexual aggression appeared in *Time* magazine. "I admire the male body and prefer to find a penis attached to it rather than having to root around in vacant lots with Ziploc bag in hand," wrote Barbara Ehrenreich. "But I'm not willing to wait another decade or two for gender peace to prevail. And if a fellow insists on using his penis as a weapon, I say that, one way or another, he ought to be swiftly disarmed."[3]

Obviously, men who commit or condone sexual violence against women should be the object of enormous anger, and women have both a moral and legal right to protect themselves against this violence. If, however, these were the only issues, the sordid Bobbitt story would have quickly faded from public awareness. The story captured the American psyche because John and Lorena Bobbitt became characters in a drama known as the American gender war, and their roles were scripted by assumptions about the relationship between sex and gender that pervade the politics of our sexual lives.

The individual who was most responsible for legitimating the modern distinction between sex and gender was the anthropologist Margaret Mead. According to the Mead doctrine, the enormous variability of human behavior in different cultural contexts suggests that innate, or biologically predetermined, behaviors are almost nonexistent in our species. Mead concluded, therefore, that the fundamental determinant of gender identity is not nature, or what we are as a result of biological inheritance, but nurture, or what we are as a result of the socialization process: "We may safely say that many if not all of the personality traits which we call masculine and feminine are as lightly linked to sex as are the clothing, the manners and the form of headdress that a society at a given period assigns to sex."[4]

During the 1960s, the Mead doctrine was incorporated into the so-called sex/gender system in feminist theory. In this system, sex refers to physiological differences in the domain of the body, and gender to learned behavior in the domain of the mind. This two-domain distinction allowed sex-specific bodies to be viewed as separate and distinct from gender-neutral minds, and legitimated the idea that biological reality is wholly independent of gender identity. As gender theoretician Sandra Lee Bartky puts it, the sex/gender system is "that complex process whereby bi-sexual infants are transformed into male and female gender personalities, the one destined to command, the other to obey."[5]

While most Americans know little and care less about feminist theory, the sex/gender system is not some arcane piece of academic jargon that has little or no effect on everyday experience. It is the most disruptive force in the politics of our sexual lives, and one of the greatest sources of division and conflict in relationships between men and women. The intent of this book is not, however, to perpetuate the gender war. It is to show that the sex/gender system is not in accord with biological reality, and that an improved understanding of the relationship between sex and gender could lead to a new standard for sexual equality that is more realistic and humane than the current standard.

This is not, however, an anti-feminist diatribe, and nowhere do I wish to imply that we should fail to celebrate the successes of the women's movement. The feminist revolution liberated untold millions of women from the shackles of male domination, and anyone who would wish to return to the dark age prior to that revolution should be either pitied or damned. And yet I will take issue with those who believe that the sex/gender system is the engine that is driving this revolution. Since there is a linkage between biological reality and gender identity, a sexually equal society will never be a gender-neutral society. If we are to achieve the goal of full sexual equality, we must, in my view, develop a standard for sexual equality premised on a very different understanding of the relationship between sex, gender, and sexual politics.

NEGATING BIOLOGICAL REALITY

In the mid-1960s, when Betty Friedan and Germaine Greer proclaimed that women were engaged in a gender war, the emphasis was on consciousness raising and fair and equitable treatment of women. In the mid-1970s, the emphasis shifted to the subordinate role of women in patriarchal culture and the need for solidarity of women in reforming that culture. The book that was most responsible for moving feminist theory in this direction was Kate Millett's *Sexual Politics*.

Since the two-domain distinction obviates the connection between biological reality and gender identity, Millett assumes that gender identity is entirely learned, or "socially constructed," in a culture dominated and controlled by men. Based on this assumption, she makes the case that politics is essentially sexual and that even so-called democracies are male hegemonies.[6] The idea that gender identity is scripted by male cultural narratives, or stories, myths, legends, and the like, "arbitrarily" invented by men to oppress women, made women's studies a growth industry. When Millett published *Sexual Politics,* the number of women's studies courses offered in American colleges and universities was fewer than twenty. That number has now grown to tens of thousands, and there are no signs that the growth is abating.

Legions of scholars have used the sex/gender system to dissect virtually every type of cultural narrative, ranging from ancient myths and legends to capitalist theory to contemporary films and advertising. The methodologies used in these studies are complex and variable, but virtually all of them are premised on the assumption that gender identity is an arbitrary cultural product that exists in the domain of mind separate and distinct from the domain of the body.

When a woman's consciousness is raised by the sex/gender system, she learns to identify herself with her gender and to see all relations with men in political terms. The menacing "other" becomes the patriarchal culture that allegedly defines her gender identity in even the most familiar and seemingly innocuous phenomena. Not surprisingly, seeing the world through the prism of the sex/gender system normally produces dramatic results. "Now that the sex/gender system has become visible to us," says gender feminist Virginia Held, "we can see it everywhere."

While most of us do not, of course, see the sex/gender system everywhere, it is everywhere present in the politics of our sexual lives. Since there is a linkage between biological reality and gender identity, the obligation to ignore this reality, or to make absent what is undeniably present, is not innocent. It has occasioned untold emotional violence in the lives of men and women, and could well be one of the least recognized and examined causes of gender confusion, marital conflict, and the high incidence of divorce.

CASUALTIES IN THE AMERICAN GENDER WAR

That the sex/gender system contributes to gender confusion is apparent in the refusal of increasing numbers of women to identify with the term *feminist*. A number of recent studies have shown that while most younger American women support feminist goals, they are reluctant to call themselves feminists. After reviewing fifty years of research on American attitudes toward gender issues and feminism, and conducting a representative survey of 2,257 adults, social scientists Leone Huddy and David Sears concluded that there is no evidence that the next generation of American women is "returning to traditionalism." While most of the younger women surveyed, those between eighteen and twenty-four, clearly embraced the goals of the feminist movement, they did not like the term feminist and refused to be identified as such.[8] As Leone Huddy sees it, "Many of them are feminist in their basic beliefs and ambitions, but they don't identify with feminism and hate the word. It connotes anger, militarism, and lesbianism."[9]

In an attempt to understand why so many American women who support feminist goals do not wish to be labeled feminists, sociologist Beth Schneider collected impressions of feminism from a diverse group of women whose ages ranged from nineteen to sixty-six. Schneider concluded that the hostility was directed at the feminist definition of and attitudes toward "normal womanhood"—sexuality, maternity, and personality traits like nurturance, warmth, and nonaggressiveness. While most of those surveyed felt that the feminist movement has done much to improve the status of women, there was general agreement that feminists are tough, aggressive, unattractive, hostile, and "afraid of being a woman."[10]

If large numbers of women refuse to deny their womanhood, or the connection between biological reality and gender identity, large numbers of men seem exceedingly confused about what manhood means. Men, as a group at least, have not been denied intellectual affirmation or been asked to sacrifice their ambitions to the demands of domestic life. As a host of male voices suggests, however, they seem to feel anything but powerful. As *Time* essayist Lance Morrow sees it, men have the growing conviction that maleness is being unfairly assailed, and that masculinity, regardless of color, has become "a bad smell in the room."[11]

Ellis Cose, in *A Man's World*, describes some of the sources of this malady: "If they [men] are married, they feel trapped between work and their families. If they are divorced fathers, they fret about being lousy dads. If they are dating, they wrestle with bewildering new rules of romantic engagement. If they are working, they are haunted by the specter of sexual harassment charges. Whatever their situation, their rights and their roles are shifting—as demands and attacks on them increase."[12]

The obvious problem with the "men have the power and women do not" equation is that it is not in accord with socioeconomic reality and the complexities of the modern world. "The mythology still among women," says psychologist Judith Sherven, "is that men have all the power, and if you're male, you must have all the power. I see it in my women clients. There is this sort of difficulty in seeing men as singular individuals, who have singular lives separate and apart from men, and a willingness to just put blanket assumptions on any man."[13]

But since men as a group are more privileged, many have been perplexed by the increasingly common spectacle of men, particularly white men, complaining of victim status. Some commentators have attributed this behavior to the "culture of complaint." Others have written it off as little more than a futile display of male resentment toward women who are now receiving the respect they have always deserved. The evidence suggests, however, that the male as victim phenomenon has more to do with gender confusion than hostility toward the feminist movement.

For example, many recent studies have shown that the majority of American men have embraced fundamental goals of the feminist movement. In a 1993 Gallup poll, 99 percent of the men said they approved of women receiving equal pay for equal work, and 88 percent favored women working outside the home regardless of family income. In spite of improvements in the lives of women over the last two decades, 52 percent of the men said that they believed society favors men over women.[14] This does not mean, of course, that we are living in a sexually equal society or that the goals of the feminist movement have been realized. Much work clearly remains to be done. It also seems clear, however, that the conflict has degenerated into a war of attrition in which the terms for peace are perpetually redefined. The principal source of this dilemma is the two-domain distinction sanctioned by the sex/gender system.

SEX, LOVE, AND MALE PATHOLOGY

Since the two-domain distinction requires that we view the behavior of men and women as entirely learned, it was reasonable to assume that the standard for healthy normalcy in love relationships should be the same for both men and women. Since women seem more capable of emotional directness and honesty, for the last twenty years social scientists have valorized women as intimacy experts and pathologized men as incapable of intimacy.

Men, said many social scientists, have a "trained incapacity to share," and have learned to overvalue independence and to fear emotional involvement. While male friendships are based on competition, emotional inhibition, and aggression, female friendships are based on emotional bonding and mutual support.[15] Given that men tend to talk about shared interests, such as sports and cars, male friendships were characterized as superficial and trivial. Since women tend to share feelings and confidences, female friendships were celebrated as deep, intimate, and true.

Social scientists also pathologized maleness because men typically view love as action, or doing things for another, while women view love as talking and acknowledging feeling. Psychotherapist Richard Driscoll in *The Binds That Tie* describes the following interaction between a married couple. After Paula asks her Don if he "really loves her," Don says, "I know I want to be married to you. I am satisfied to go to work every morning, because I know that I am supporting you and that you are there for me. I would never want to leave you, and I would never want you to leave me. Is that what you mean by love?" Hurt and angered by this response, Paula says, "But why can't you say you love me?" Driscoll then points out that Don, unfortunately, has been taught to view love as action whereas Paula has been taught to view love properly—as feeling.[16]

But for reasons that will soon become obvious, the action versus feeling view of love tends to be quite real in the lives of men and women. In one recent study, seven couples were asked to record their marital activities and marital satisfaction for several days.[17] Each spouse was asked to note on a daily basis when the other did something helpful, like cleaning or fixing a broken chair, when affection was expressed, and the degree of satisfaction in the marriage. The wives were most satisfied when their husbands verbally expressed affection regardless of what the husbands did for them. The husbands, in contrast, were most satisfied when their wives acted on their behalf, regardless of affectionate words.

How do we account for this discrepancy in the language of love? It is, say the social scientists, entirely a product of learning. As psychologist Carol Tavris puts it, "The doing-versus-talking distinction in the emotional styles of males and females begins in childhood, when boys begin to develop what psychologists call 'side by side' relationships, in which intimacy means sharing the same activity—sports, games, watching a movie or a sports event together." Girls, in contrast, "tend to prefer 'face to face' relationships, in which intimacy means revealing ideas and emotions in a heart-to-heart exchange."[18]

A number of social scientists contend that the pathology of maleness is painfully obvious in male humor. The tendency of men to joke with verbal put downs that women often perceive as aggressive and hostile is not, they say, a sign of mental health. It serves, says psychologist Scott Swain, to "camouflage the hidden agenda of closeness."[19] Or as Tavris puts it, "men use jokes to create distance and express anger and contempt. Most men become fluent in joke-speak and its many meanings by adolescence. They know that "What a jerk!," coming from a friend when they fall off a bicycle, conveys amused affection, but the same remark from a passing stranger is an act of hostility."[20]

That men tend to respond to depression with actions, like frantic work, driving around, and compulsive and excessive exercise, is viewed as yet another sign of male pathology. How do we account for this behavior? Social scientist Catherine Reismann claims that the "culturally approved idioms of men" result in the "distancing of the self from feelings of sadness," and an inability to recognize helplessness, and vulnerability.[21] The fact that men often use action metaphors to describe depression, like "something's got to give," "pushing it," and "running wide open," is also considered a learned avoidance strategy.

Male pathology, the social scientists contend, is also evident in the manner in which men tend to feel close to one another. When twenty-six men were asked to describe the "most meaningful occasion spent with the same-sex friend, twenty of the twenty-six events involved "an activity other than talking," such as fishing, playing guitars, driving, and weightlifting. Why do men associate action with closeness? Since men, claim social scientists, learn that expressing emotions directly is a sign of weakness and lack of self-control, action is a means of feigning closeness without being required to disclose personal feelings. Masculine norms for maleness also account, claim social scientists, for the reluctance of men to openly express grief. "Often," says psychologist Ron Taffel, "a man's own suffering so threatens his idealized masculine self-identity that he cannot even admit to pain."[22]

Many social scientists argue that one area where the pathologized male is "allowed" to express emotions is as participant and spectator in sports. "In sports, many of the usual prohibitions on males are lifted," comments psychotherapist Bernie Zilbergeld. "A man can be as emotional and expressive about his favorite team and players as he wants. . . . There's even a lot of physical contact: back-and butt-slapping, shoulder and arm touching, and hugging. Sports is the one place where men can safely become boys again, where they can drop the facade of Mr. Up-Tight-And-In-Control and just play."[23]

Since much of what we are as men and women is a product of learning, many of the behaviors in the litany of male pathology are cultural products and subject to change. But since the expectation that men must think, feel, and behave like women in love relationships is not in accord with biological reality, the social and psychological consequences have been nothing short of disastrous. Consider, for example, the primary reason why women seek a divorce.

When divorced women are asked to explain the failure of a marriage, the common refrain is "lack of communication," or the ex-husband's unwillingness to talk about or share feelings.[24] In one recent study, over two thirds of the women surveyed felt that men would never understand them, or that the men in their lives would remain forever clueless about the lives of women.[25] Yet numerous studies have also shown that women view men who deviate from the masculine norm by displaying and talking openly about emotions as "too feminine" and "poorly adjusted."[26]

SEX-SPECIFIC DIFFERENCES
IN THE HUMAN BRAIN

The Mead doctrine occasioned a revolution in our thinking about gender identity for the same reasons that the theories of Copernicus, Darwin, and Einstein occasioned revolutions in thought. It was derived in accordance with research methodologies and rules of evidence designed to produce objective and value-free knowledge. Although a large body of research on sex-specific behavior that could not be explained by learning per se began to accumulate not long after the doctrine was formulated, this evidence appeared "soft" in the absence of biological explanations. We now know that the biological factors that contribute to these behaviors are differing levels of sex hormones and sex-specific differences in the human brain.

Much of our knowledge about the sex-specific human brain was derived from postmortem dissections and studies of brain-damaged patients as compared with those of normal subjects. It is, however, studies that rely on computer-based imaging systems that have provided the most dramatic evidence that male and female brains process information differently. These systems generate three-dimensional images of the brains of conscious subjects, and indicate which brain regions are implicated in the performance of specific cognitive tasks.

Studies based on this technology indicate that language functions tend to be localized in different regions of the brains of men and women. This contributes to sex-specific discrepancies in language fluency, associational fluency, and verbal reasoning. Other sex-specific differences in the two hemispheres of the neocortex also contribute to discrepancies in communication styles. When men and women tend to solve problems differently, perceive different sets of relevant details, and display different orientations toward objects and movements in three-dimensional space, this is not merely learned behavior. These habits of mind are conditioned by sex-specific differences in the human brain.

The sex-specific human brain also impacts all aspects of the human sensorium. As a result, men and women tend to display disparate levels of sensitivity to touch, taste, odors, and sounds. There are also sex-specific differences in the area of visual field where vision is sharpest, in peripheral vision, and in night vision.

That differences in the brains of men and women have behavioral consequences is also apparent in studies of people living in very diverse human cultures. Behaviors associated with the differences emerge shortly after birth and become more prevalent throughout infancy, childhood, and adolescence. Similar patterns of sex-specific behavior are apparent in the same-sex games of children, and the interactions between players in all human cultures. This is also true in flirtation behavior, nonverbal signs of growing sexual intimacy, and courtship rituals.

Neuroscience has also provided bold new insights into an aspect of our lives where the attempt to ignore or transcend differences occasions the most confusion and conflict—romantic love relationships. There are chemicals in our brains, called neurotransmitters, that make the experience of eros far more universal than we previously imagined. Normally produced at various stages in love relationships, these chemicals occasion similar emotional and physical states in all human organisms.

The states range from amphetamine-like highs to opiate-like calms, and a sudden drop in the levels of some neurotransmitters can cause withdrawal symptoms like those of mind-altering drugs. The excitement of falling in love, the tendency to suffer depression when love is lost, the difference between erotic and companionate love, and even the high incidence of divorce around the fourth year of marriage can now be better understood in terms of levels and types of neurotransmitters.

What is quite clear in this research is that sexual differences are not confined to the domain of the mind; they also exist in the domain of the body. This does not mean, as the male chauvinists and misogynists among us would probably like to believe, that gender differences are in the same class as sexual differences. It does, however, force us to conclude that men and women have been living for the past thirty years with the absurd expectation that moral and political correctness demands gender sameness.

Since behavioral tendencies associated with the s/he brain cannot be obviated by learning, there is a definite relationship between biological reality and gender identity. When we examine that relationship, the results are startling. Many of the behaviors social scientists recognize as sign and symbol of male pathology are associated with the sex-specific male brain. And many of the alleged inadequacies of women who fail to think, feel, and behave the same as men are associated with sex-specific differences in the female brain. The good news is that research on the sex-specific human brain can liberate us from much of the confusion and conflict in the politics of our sexual lives. The bad news is that the potential for sexist abuses of this knowledge is enormous.

THE DANGERS OF DIFFERENCE

When the discovery was made a century ago that a woman's brain was smaller on average than a man's, at least a dozen men of science argued that this difference accounted for the emotional weakness and intellectual inferiority of women. After it was understood that sex-specific brain size was merely a function of body weight, male scientists alleged that women were intellectually inferior to men because their brains have smaller frontal lobes and larger parietal lobes.

Following speculation that the parietal lobes are associated with higher level cognitive processes, these same scientists reported that those lobes in female brains were smaller than previous research indicated.[27]

More recently, the so-called evolutionary biologists have alleged that the human brain has evolved customized mental mechanisms[28] for fundamental aspects of experience, particularly sexuality and mating. The alleged mechanisms, say these theorists, explain why women are drawn to mates with status and resource, why they prefer more reckless and extravagant men during brief affairs, and why they are drawn to more conservative men when seeking a long-term relationship.

This picture of women as vessels and vassals scheming to balance the desire for sexual gratification against the compulsion to find a suitable mate stands in bold contrast to the picture of men. According to the evolutionary biologists, mental mechanisms compel males to be attracted to physically youthful and attractive females, particularly to those whose hips are roughly a third larger than their waist. And why do men settle for less than attractive women when playing the field? They are driven by mental mechanisms.

If the material on the sex-specific human brain is a bit challenging, there are good reasons to accept this challenge. Given the long history of sexist abuses of scientific knowledge, knowing something about what science actually says about the sex-specific human brain is not a mere entertainment or intellectual exercise. It is an essential weapon in the fight against sexism and in the quest for full sexual equality.

As we shall see, nothing in this research argues for a causal linkage between sex-specific brains and gender-specific behavior. Every human brain is unique, becomes more so as a result of learning, and there is more variation between same-sex brains than opposite-sex brains. Nature plays a larger role in fashioning human sexual identity and behavior than the two-domain distinction allowed. But since nurture remains a vital part of the equation, what we are as men and women is massively conditioned by learning and subject to change.

The fact that female and male brains tend to process information differently lends no support to facile over-generalizations reinforcing negative stereotypes of either sex. Anyone who claims otherwise is suffering from either ignorance or sexism, or both. We must be able to remind such people that the overlap between neuronal organization and function in the brains of men and women is enormous, and that behavioral tendencies associated with the on-average differences have as many disadvantages as advantages. Most important, there is not a shred of evidence that any single individual, whether male or female, should feel restricted in the performance of any task or in the pursuit of any goal. Yet the greatest danger here is not, in my view, sexist abuses of this knowledge.

THE S/HE BRAIN
AND SEX DISCRIMINATION LAW

When scientific knowledge enters the public domain, ex-trascientific variables normally play a large role in determining how this knowledge is assimilated. As we assimilate the research on the sex-specific human brain, the cultural variables that could lead to the most disastrous consequences are two terms for defining gender identity that are foundational to our current standard for sexual equality—the law of the excluded middle and the two domain distinction.

The law of the excluded middle derives from Aristotle's three basic laws of thought. The first law states that x is x, or that everything is or is not something else. The second defines contradiction as a violation of the premise that x cannot be both y and not y, meaning that the same attribute cannot both belong and not belong to the same subject at the same time and in the same respect. And the third law, known as the excluded middle, says that x is either y or is not y, or that an attribute does or does not belong to a subject. The manner in which this logic informs our constructions of sexual differences is straightforward—an essential attribute of one sex does not apply to the other, contradiction arises when we attempt to do so, and there is no middle ground between these attributes.

While the sex/gender system is intended to obviate appeals to biological reality in dealing with gender issues, it is premised on the same logic we use in dealing with sexual differences. And since the law of the excluded middle was linked to the two-domain distinction in sex discrimination law, this law sanctions an enormous amount of legal violence against women. Under the equal protection clause of the Fourteenth Amendment to the Constitution, any rule of practice that draws a gender line must correspond with the reality of gender and must not be intended to discriminate. And given that standards for equality are comparative in sex discrimination law, appeals for equal treatment are decided on the basis of "empirical similarity."

As Catherine MacKinnon puts it, "For differential treatment to be discriminatory, the sexes must be similarly situated by legislation, qualifications, circumstance or physical endowment. This applies to sex the broader legal norm of neutrality, the law's version of objectivity. To test for gender neutrality, reverse the sexes and compare. To see if a women is discriminated against on the basis of sex, ask if a similarly situated man would be or was so treated."[29]

While the usual explanation for this absurd predicament is that it perpetuates male dominance structures and hierarchies, consider the roles played by the two-domain distinction and the law of the excluded middle. The distinction disallowed the prospect of appealing to biological differences to discriminate against women. But since the law of the excluded middle deals only in categorical oppositions, or does not allow for the predicate of sameness, there was no logical basis for providing equal protection for differences in biological roles and functions.

"As a concept," writes UCLA law professor Christine Littleton, "equality suffers from a 'mathematical fallacy'— that is, the view that only things that are the same can ever be equal."[30] The fallacy sanctions the view that since women are, or could be, like men, an egalitarian society is one in which women are treated the same as men. The two-domain distinction also explains why women have been reluctant to demand that equal protection be extended to biological differences. Since recognition of these differences would undermine the assumption, the right be treated "equally," or the same as men, would be threatened.

If sex discrimination law dealt only in the realms of the moral or philosophical, research on the sex-specific brain would not be an issue. What makes the research a large issue is the fact that those who administer this law are obliged to recognize empirical measures of sameness, and the privileged authority on such measures is science. Obviously, this makes for an ominous prospect—the male "same" against which difference is measured in sex discrimination could be extended beyond the sex-specific male body to include behavioral tendencies associated with the sex-specific male brain. This could occur in spite of the fact that we already sanction an enormous amount of violence against women by failing to provide equal protection for roles and functions associated with the female body.

Fortunately, the research clearly indicates that sex-specific differences in the brains of men and women are not in the same class as sexual differences. What is required to understand the differences is an alternative logical framework in which sameness, or the enormous overlap of cognitive and emotional processes along the entire continuum of human behavior, is the predicate for defining differences. The logic that performs this feat, which was originally developed by the Danish scientist Niels Bohr in an effort to deal with wave-particle dualism in quantum physics, is the logical framework of complementarity.

What is most remarkable about this framework is that it provides an empirically valid basis for implementing a new and improved standard for sexual equality. This is, I realize, a bold statement that should not be taken at face value. But as I hope to make clear, the new understanding of the relationship between sex and gender makes no logical, or moral, sense in the absence of complementarity.

In order to maximize the benefits and minimize the dangers of this research, we must, in my view, implement a new standard for sexual equality based on the logical framework of complementarity. I am also convinced that the group that is best situated in terms of numbers, intellectual talents, and overall influence to implement the new standard is the feminist movement. If the movement is to undertake this formidable task, however, feminists must be willing to accept a very disturbing proposition—the two-domain distinction is false, and the sex/gender system that is foundational to second-wave feminist theory is not in accord with biological reality.

BRAIN SCIENCE AND FEMINIST THEORY

While the feminist movement remains a formidable presence in American colleges and universities, this does not appear to be the case in the larger society. The essential dilemma is that second-wave feminist theory has become increasingly more diverse, fragmented, and divisive as particular constituencies have sought to fashion theories that fit their political agendas. Also, while second-wave feminist theory has always alleged that the reality of women is scripted by patriarchal narratives, the tendency to divide the reality of men and women into two hostile and warring camps has become increasingly more pronounced.

One unfortunate result is that second-wave feminist theory tends to obviate the prospect that men and women can engage in a meaningful dialogue about issues of sexual equality without recourse to blame and anger. Another is the tendency of feminists to brand other feminists who deviate from the dictates of particular theories as male collaborators. Consequently, many women who would otherwise have remained powerful allies of the feminist movement have become disaffected.

The situation is further exacerbated by the fact that the increasingly rarefied debate over feminist theory in the academy has become more isolated from political realities in the outside world. Since much of this debate is based on poststructuralist methodology, the attempt to "subvert binary constructions of gender" has resulted in a denaturalization of both sex and gender. The methodology presumably allows women to "celebrate their unbounded freedom to proliferate multiple identities in a wide range of discursive practices." But since it also eliminates the category "woman" as a coherent and stable subject in feminist theory, the result, as philosopher Richard Rorty puts it, is that "theory" is sacrificed in "favor of fantasying. There is no moral to these fantasies, nor any public (pedagogic or political) use to be made of them."[31]

The triumph of poststructuralism has further undermined the solidarity of the feminist movement by contributing to the success of identity politics. Rather than present critical challenges to the structures of inequality, those who practice identity politics examine the logic of interest group politics in competition for a larger share of resources. When this becomes the goal of feminist theory, the result, says Kathleen Jones, is "the rise of new forms of nationalism and heart-wrenching territorial wars within feminism. Feminists have become captured by the same political discourse that prevents Zionists from ever even listening to the P.L.O., and that cuts off dialogue between members of the Ulster Party and the I.R.A. We have established 'pass laws' in feminism."[32]

In the chapter on second-wave feminist theory, I will attempt to demonstrate that the sex/gender system is the greatest single source of the deep divisions and conflicts in the feminist movement. If this demonstration is as devastating as I believe it to be, it will not endear me to my feminist friends and colleagues. The fact that I have been an avid supporter of the woman's movement for all of my adult life will probably do little to assuage their anger and resentment. The intent is not, however, to launch an ill-mannered attack on feminist theory. Rather, it is to revitalize the feminist movement.

MAPPING THE JOURNEY

What is most significant about the evolution of the human brain is that it allowed human reality to be represented and perpetuated in complex language systems. Most of this discussion focuses on developing an understanding of how the sex-specific human brain contributes to differences in the linguistic realities of men and women for an obvious reason. Much of the confusion and conflict in the American gender war is due to a failure to understand that the languages used by men and women tend to be sex specific.

When our forebears walked upright through the grasslands of East Africa 4 million years ago, their brain size was roughly half our own, and the level of their conscious awareness was comparable to that of modern chimpanzees. Over millions of years natural selection favored the survival of bigger brained ancestors, and cognition played an increasingly larger role in mate selection. The effects of mate selection on the evolution of gender-specific differences in lower brain regions conditioned the evolution of the more recently evolved neocortex.

Since the brain regions that underwent the greatest expansion are associated with language use, it seems logical that there would be a correlation between increased brain size and more complex behavior and artifacts. There is, however, no evidence of this in the fossil records. While we do witness higher levels of complexity in material culture, migratory patterns, and social behavior, these signs of enhanced cognition are very marginal in comparison with the dramatic increases in brain size.

Even after the brain of our species reached the modern average 100,000 years ago, our forebears do not seem to have possessed any particular survival advantages. Moreover, there are no indications that their descendants would become the architects of something as grand as human civilization. But then something quite remarkable happened. Fossil records from 40,000 years ago testify to the rapid emergence of human civilization and to the extraordinary creativity and insight of human beings. The explanation for this sudden and incredibly recent appearance of fully human ancestors is as simple as it is startling. The human brain began to construct reality based on the complex symbol system of language a scant 70,000 years ago at most.

Over the vast reaches of time before this momentous event, our ancestors lived in small tribes where men were hunters and women were gatherers. Since the terms of survival for male hunters and female gatherers were quite different, natural selection favored the evolution of disparate emotional and cognitive processes in the brains of men and women. What science has to say about the alternative ways in which information is processed in the s/he brain is fascinating, and allows us to understand why the communication styles, interests, and expectations of men and women tend to diverge.

The greatest challenge here is not to develop a working understanding of differences between the brains of men and women. It is to properly evaluate the relative influence of nature and nurture in the bewilderingly complex tapestry of human behavior. If the threads of nature and nurture are separated, the tapestry unravels into tangled heaps, and the resulting misconceptions are the stuff out of which sexist abuses of scientific knowledge are made.

CHAPTER 2

The Making of Love's Body: Evolution and the Sexes

Urge and urge and urge,
Always the procreant urge of the world.

Out of the dimness opposite equals advance, always substance
    and increase, always sex,
Always a knit of identity, always distinction, always a breed of life.
                                        —WALT WHITMAN
                                        "Song of Myself"

Since evolution deals in whole organisms, understanding what science says about the evolution of the s/he brain must also include the body. At the point at which our ancestors emerged as a species distinct from the primates roughly 7 million years ago, they were still moving about on both hind and forelimbs in the dense primeval forests of East Africa. The forebears who wandered the vast savanna plains 4 million years ago walked upright. Also moving through this sea of grassland were herds of ancient varieties of gazelles, wildebeests, elands, bushbuck, and zebras. Stalking these herds were ancestral lions, cheetahs, and feral dogs—the big game hunters of this age.[33]

The adult brains of these distant relatives, whose maximal height was 4 feet, were comparable in size to those of modern chimpanzees. Perhaps they hooted at one another to signal the discovery of fields of seeds, nestling birds, ostrich eggs, or baby antelopes. But they were incapable of anything resembling a conversation, and the repertoire of their behaviors was limited. Mating rituals were probably no more complicated than those of modern primates, and levels of self-awareness were minimal. Nothing suggests that these lowly scavengers would become an evolutionary success, much less that their descendants would rule the earth and journey to the stars.

After the hands were freed as a result of upright posture, mutations that allowed the hands to become more adept at manipulating objects became selectively advantageous. Upright posture also led to the repositioning of female sexual anatomy to enhance face-to-face coitus. Human females have a downward-tilting vagina, as opposed to the backward oriented vulva of primates. This makes face-to-face coitus more comfortable, and allows the male pelvic bone to rub against and more effectively stimulate the clitoris. While orangutans, pygmy chimps, and gorillas occasionally have intercourse facing one another, there is nothing in their sexual anatomy that makes this position more pleasurable or easier to assume.

After face-to-face coitus became the habitual mode of intercourse, the bases for sexual attraction gradually became more refined and selective. Faces are the most expressive feature of our anatomy, and sexual partners who look into one another's faces are often engaged in elaborate nonverbal communication. One legacy of this development is dilated pupils as a sign of sexual attraction. Another is the tendency to view faces and eyes as indicators of intelligence, creativity, and insight. The increased importance of facial expressions also added new cognitive dimensions to the ancestral mating game, and put a higher premium on intelligence in the selection of mates.

Another consequence of bigger human brains is well known by any woman who has experienced childbirth. The head of human infants is so large that delivery is prolonged, painful, and often life threatening. Yet the brains of our ancestors continued to expand after the heads of infants reached the maximal size where mothers could survive delivery. How could this be? Scientists speculate that minor mutations in regulatory genes during the period from a million to 200,000 years ago slowed down and greatly extended the maturation process of human children.[34] As a result, the period during which the brains of infants grow outside the womb became much longer. Just how dramatic this development was can be illustrated in a comparison between human and chimpanzee offspring.

The embryos of chimpanzees and human beings are identical in the early stages, and there is a large resemblance between the head and bodies of each in infancy. Yet the chimpanzee at birth has 40 percent of its total cranial capacity, while the human infant is born with only 23 percent. Similarly, chimpanzees acquire the chemical responses of the liver, immune system, kidneys, digestive tract, and motor tract shortly after birth, while the human infant does not achieve this level of maturation until after six to nine months.[35] Also, chimpanzees reach adulthood at age ten, while human beings are often not fully mature until age twenty.

Immature babies were an enormous reproductive burden on ancestral females living, until quite recently, in hunter-gatherer tribes perpetually on the move. Children were nursed and often carried during the first four years of life, and even the most precocious child could not forage and adequately feed itself until it was a teenager. In this situation survival for mother and children was highly dependent on the presence of a father who could provide food and participate in child rearing on a steady basis.

The prolonged maturation of the human brain outside the womb is also the key to understanding a critical difference between ourselves and other species. Virtually all other species survived by becoming specialists, while we survived by becoming generalists. Although animals, particularly our primate cousins, are capable of foresight, planning, and learning, the vast majority of animal behaviors are genetically programmed. In other words, an environmental stimulus invokes a particular response, and little or no training is required.

In our case very few behaviors are genetically programmed, and an enormous amount of training is necessary to make us even minimally functional. It was this ability to learn free from the constraints of genetically determined behaviors that was the key to survival. Since the immature brain of a human infant is very malleable and plastic, vast amounts of information can be encoded in its expanding neuronal organization during the maturation process.

UNIQUE ASPECTS
OF THE HUMAN MATING GAME

The powerful bonding between mates that is required to raise children was enhanced by another unique feature of human sexuality—concealed ovulation. Most mammals copulate when the female is in estrus, or ovulating and capable of fertilization, and are sexually inactive most of the time. Female mammals often present or display their genitals to males during estrus, and seem aware that they are ovulating. In female primates the vagina, as well as buttocks and breasts in some species, swell and change color during estrus, leaving little doubt that the time for procreation is at hand. From an evolutionary perspective, this makes good sense. Since copulation makes animals vulnerable to predators, consumes valuable calories, and prevents food gathering, getting the job done quickly with a high probability of success is the optimal way to perpetuate genotype in phenotype.[36]

Based on these criteria, we are an evolutionary disaster in reproductive terms. A human female can be sexually receptive throughout her menstrual cycle and, aside from a few easily overlooked biological changes, there are no overt signs when ovulation occurs. Getting pregnant is also complicated by the fact that ovulation cycles in human females vary, and sexual drive does not, as it does in primates, radically increase during ovulation.[37] A high correlation between copulation and conception is not part of this equation. Most human copulations do not result in pregnancy, and there is only a 28 percent probability that males and females copulating at maximal rates during a single menstrual cycle will conceive a child.[38]

The impacts of concealed ovulation on the sexual lives of our forebears are easily imagined. A male who is obliged to copulate with a female on a regular basis to conceive a child would be more inclined to provide food and protection. Less obvious and more interesting, the loss by ancestral females of the compulsion to copulate during estrus probably gave them more control over their sexual desires and more freedom in the choice of mates. As females became more empowered to choose the males with whom they had sexual intercourse, cortical control became a larger factor in the mating game for both sexes.

Another bit of weirdness about human sexuality is that all other group-living animals, whether promiscuous or monogamous, have sex in public while we have sex in private. The penchant for private sex may have emerged not long after the loss of estrus among ancestral females. More intimacy in sexual intercourse, as well as a more possessive and proprietary attitude toward a sexual partner, probably created a need for privacy.

If we assume that our ancestors were at least as promiscuous as we are today and that their infidelities also occasioned conflict, private promiscuous sex would be less likely to cause disruptions in a closely knit community of hunter-gatherers. Private sex also requires some rudimentary decision making and planning, not to mention occasional deception and guile. This would enhance mating between those with greater intelligence.

MY BODY IS MADE FOR YOUR BODY

The role of enhanced cognition in mate selection is also apparent in the physically attractive traits associated with our sex-specific bodies. Human hair follicles indicate that we, like the primates, were once covered with hair. Since the exposure of tender areas on the chest and groin probably enhanced sexual pleasure, those ancestral males and females who lost hair in these areas as a result of mutation were probably attracted to one another.

It also seems likely that females who had less hair on their face, lips, and breasts were more responsive to stimulation in these areas, and more inclined to engage in sexual intercourse. But why were males drawn to females with smooth faces and softer, mellifluous voices, and females drawn to males with beards and deep voices? Perhaps males found females with exposed faces and sweet voices less threatening, and females found males with deep voices and beards stronger and more mature.[39]

The breasts of human females are another oddity in our sexual anatomy. The breasts of female primates enlarge only during lactation, while those of human females are permanently enlarged. If the intent were to design breasts optimally suited for survival, evolution does not receive high marks here. Human female breasts bounce painfully when women run, are extremely sensitive to abrasive contact, and can obstruct vision in bending over to collect food. Human infants are more easily fed from a bottle-sized teat than a slippery, rounded teat, and can even be suffocated by the large breasts of their mothers. Why did these breasts evolve? Although there are a number of theories, none is particularly compelling. All we can state with any confidence is that ancestral males were more attracted to big-busted females.

Another intriguing aspect of human sexuality is female orgasm. Even though the female primate possesses a clitoris, and has been observed in captivity to self-stimulate to orgasm, female primate orgasm during copulation is rare.[40] Once again evolution displays its usual pragmatism. Female primates have a large compulsion to copulate during estrus, and orgasm is not a prerequisite for conception. Yet human females are not only capable of experiencing orgasm on a fairly regular basis; they also have the capacity for multiple orgasms.

How does mate selection account for this particular violation of pragmatism? Ancestral males whose sexual partners were capable of the tumultuous emotional experience of orgasm would not only be more sexually stimulated themselves, they would also be more assured that the gratified female would not seek sex from other males.[41] This makes more sense when we consider that female orgasm triggers the release of neurotransmitters associated with feelings that encourage bonding, such as calm, tenderness, and attachment. We must also consider a more prosaic biological explanation. Since a female satiated by orgasm is more likely to remain lying down after the male has ejaculated into her vaginal canal, there is a greater likelihood that male sperm will reach and fertilize the ovum.[42]

If female orgasm was selectively advantageous for mate selection and impregnation, then it would seem that all surviving human females would climax during intercourse. How, then, do we account for the fact that this is not the case? One interesting possibility is that orgasm among ancestral females functioned as a preconscious exam for mate selection. Women are more likely to have orgasm with sexually attentive and attractive husbands than with sexually atten-

tive and attractive secret lovers. Similarly, call girls with a
steady and considerate clientele have orgasm more frequently than streetwalkers who often have sex with complete
strangers. If women are more relaxed and sexually receptive
to men who display qualities conducive to developing long-
term relationships, orgasm would be one indicator of those
qualities.[43]

One feature of female sexual anatomy indicates that the
desire of males to possess, dominate, and control females has
a very long history. There is no equivalent of the human
female hymen in chimps, gorillas, and orangutans, and there
is no evolutionarily valid reason for its existence. This cres-
cent-shaped flap of membrane blocking the entrance to the
vagina probably originated as a minor birth defect similar to
those that produce webbed fingers or toes. In addition to
being utterly useless, intercourse with a female with an intact
hymen ruptures this membrane and causes pain and bleed-
ing. How did this biological perversity spread through the
human gene pool? It provided jealous males with unmistakable and brutal assurance of female virginity.[44]

According to male locker room wisdom, a man with a
large penis and testes is more likely to sexually gratify his
partner. But since the clitoris is stimulated to orgasm by the
angle and movement of a penis, a larger than average penis
is not needed for this purpose. Also, intercourse with a male
whose penis is unusually large in the erect state can be
painful for many females. This explains why women do not
swoon in the presence of huge male genitalia as men tend to
do in the presence of big female breasts.

If ancestral females were not attracted to males with large
penises and testes, how did the comparatively large genitalia
of human males evolve? The answer is that males in species
that copulate more frequently have larger genitalia, while
those in species that copulate less frequently have smaller
genitalia. Male chimps, who live in a sexual nirvana of
promiscuous females, copulate with greater frequency than

human males. Consequently, their penis and testes, relative to body weight, are larger than those of human males. A 100-pound male chimpanzee has 4-ounce testes, as opposed to the 1.5-ounce average for human males, and an erect penis measuring roughly 3 inches.

Rate of copulation also explains why a 450-pound male gorilla has testes that weigh less than those of an average man, and an erect penis only 1.25 inches in length. Gorilla genitalia are small relative to body weight because even a successful male with a harem of three or four females has sex only a few times a year. The exclusive access that a gorilla has to females in his harem during estrus ensures that a small contribution of sperm will result in offspring.[45]

BIGGER BRAINS
AND THE ORIGINS OF LANGUAGE

Although life for virtually all of our evolutionary history was brutish and short, the ancestral men and women whose genes survived in subsequent generations were, in retrospect, engaged in a very grand enterprise. We will never write a complete history on the origins of the complex symbol system of language, but our improved understanding of the evolution of brain regions associated with language use has provided important clues. The evidence suggests that beginning roughly a million years ago, gestures used to focus attention on aspects of the environment were displaced by vocalizations. But this signaling system did not allow for conversation, or for the generation of new meanings with word symbols that others could understand.

The development of a complex language system required greater differentiation between cognitive tasks performed by the left and right hemispheres of the brain, which control opposite sides of the body. Language in people with normal hemispheric dominance, meaning virtually all right handers and two-thirds of left handers, is localized predominantly in the left hemisphere. A recent study of Stone Age tools indicates that their makers were disproportionately right handed. This suggests that the left hemispheric dominance required for complex language development may have begun to evolve as early as 2 million years ago.[46]

In the fossil remains, we also witness dramatic increases over the last 2 million years in the size of other brain areas associated with language use. During this period the human neocortex, which is intimately connected with linguistic functions, doubled in size. Portions of the human brain dedicated to linguistic functions, such as Broca's area (involved in producing the sounds of speech) and Wernicke's area (involved in the selection of appropriate words and phrases) also visibly expanded. Equally important, changes in the human vocal apparatus allowed a complex range of sounds to be articulated.

The larynx is a membrane that covers the opening to the trachea, and its primary function is to prevent food and other particles from getting into the lungs. The human larynx is positioned relatively deep in the neck, and is roughly horizontal in relation to the tongue and the esophagus, or the tube that extends into the stomach. Since this arrangement requires that food pass over the horizontal larynx to reach the esophagus, it increases the likelihood of choking. Yet it also allows the tongue to manipulate air in the mouth to produce a range of vowels and consonants.

THE GREAT LEAP FORWARD:
BRAIN BECOMES MIND

The emergence of a language system that allows for the expression of an unlimited range of meanings was incredibly recent and sudden. Prior to 70,000 years ago, when our ancestors had not yet migrated out of Africa, there is no indication in the fossil remains that such a language system was in use. During this same period another species of hominids, the heavily muscled and shorter Neanderthals, lived in Europe and western Asia. For reasons we do not fully understand, these close relatives on the family tree, like 99 percent of the species that have existed on this planet, became extinct about 35,000 years ago.

When we examine the artifacts produced by our forebears 70,000 years ago, there is good reason to wonder why we did not suffer that fate as well. The stone tools used by our modern-looking African ancestors are primitive, display little innovation, and are similar to those used by the very unmodern-looking Neanderthals. There were no unequivocal compound tools, such as a wooden handle with an axelike blade, and no variations in tool making in different geographical locations. Even though there is only a very marginal difference between these people and ourselves in bodies, brains, and genes, the differences in behavior are enormous.

But then, in a mere heartbeat of evolutionary time, there appeared in France and Spain 40,000 years ago a people whose cultural artifacts grandly testify to their creativity and intelligence. Compound tools, standardized bone and antler tools, and tools that fall into distinct categories or functions, such as mortars and pestles, needles, rope, and fishhooks, appear in the fossil remains. Also found in these remains are weapons designed to kill large animals at a distance—darts, barbed harpoons, bows and arrows, and spear throwers.

Other artifacts suggest that human life had become more than a brutal struggle to survive. Rock paintings, necklaces, pendants, fired-clay ceramic sculptures, flutes, and rattles are indicative of profound aesthetic preoccupations and religious impulses. Equally interesting, the languages and cultures of people living in geographically disparate places become after this point in time increasingly more unique and disparate.

Why was human civilization born so suddenly following a gestation period of millions of years, and without any prior indications that this momentous event was about to occur? Part of the explanation is obvious—a new and far more sophisticated language system made it possible to symbolically represent and manipulate reality in ideas and constructs arranged in time sequence. In short, our ancestors began to converse as we converse.

How can we explain the emergence of this new language in such a meteoric fashion? The best explanation is that minor mutations resulted in one or both of the following: (1) changes in the neuronal organization and communication pathways of the brain that greatly enhanced linguistic abilities; (2) alterations in larynx, tongue, and associated muscles that permitted the full range of vowels and consonants to be articulated.

The intimate connection between our evolutionary past and the ability of the human brain to construct reality based on the complex symbol system of language can be illustrated by an experiment in which an infant is placed in any of the cultures where one or more of 2,796 extant human languages are spoken. All of these languages have the following in common: a large number of meaningful symbols (words) can be generated from a small set of basic sounds (phonemes), and the word symbols can be used to construct an unlimited number of sentences based on a finite set of rules (grammar).

Yet the differences between language systems are often so enormously complex that a trained linguist can easily devote a lifetime to understanding the nuances of a particular language. In spite of these large differences, the child in our experiment would assimilate whatever language system(s) he or she is exposed to with ease and very minimal training. What accounts for the staggering linguistic abilities of the child is a large brain adapted for the acquisition and use of language that continues to grow and mature outside the womb.

Even a four-day-old infant can discriminate between the voice of the mother and another woman of the same age, between a natural flow of speech and words spoken in isolated sequence, and between the language spoken by the mother and another language.[47] When a child is eight to ten months old, it will begin to babble, or to utter syllables in an apparently meaningless fashion. Soon thereafter the child will utter words with phonemes like those used in the linguistic environment.[48] At about age six or seven, the mechanisms that have evolved to assimilate language begin to shut down, and the neuronal organization associated with language use becomes far less malleable.

LANGUAGE, SYMBOLIC UNIVERSES, AND SEXUAL POLITICS

When our ancestors began to construct reality based on the complex symbol system of language, they did not merely acquire a tool that allowed experience to be coordinated in vastly more efficient ways. They became empowered to create and transform themselves in a symbolic universe in which all aspects of reality are linguistically based constructions. Prior to the point at which this universe came into existence, learning involved little more than emulating a limited range of behaviors dictated by the terms of survival.

Following the emergence of a fully developed language system, as the rich and varied material cultures that existed in France and Spain 40,000 years ago attest, learned behaviors became associated with linguistically constructed roles within various domains of social reality. In each of these domains, roles were defined in terms of institutional frameworks, such as family and work. Given that faithful performance of roles was essential for survival, the duties and obligations associated with roles could not be viewed as arbitrary human inventions subject to change. The mechanism that sacredly legitimated and integrated all aspects of symbolic universes was mytho-religious thought.

Since females were necessarily dependent on males when pregnant and rearing children, the roles played by women were constrained by procreative functions. While the roles of males were similarly constrained by superior upper body strength and higher levels of aggression, these attributes, minus the difference in reproductive burdens, favored dominance of males over females. This dominance conferred upon males the opportunity to fashion symbolic universes that are more commensurate with constructions of reality in the sex-specific male brain. There is, of course, nothing sacrosanct about the structure of these symbolic universes. They merely attest to the fact that unequal power relations conferred a grossly unfair advantage on males.

Yet the sex-specific human brain is not a tabula rasa or blank template on which cultural narratives are scripted or imprinted. When men and women learn cultural narratives, they tend to construct these narratives differently owing to innate on-average differences in the s/he brain. If this is the case, the two-domain distinction sanctioned by the sex/gender system is invalid. The same applies to two major assumptions that are everywhere present in the American gender war—cultural narratives were exclusively invented by men to oppress and control women; and the gender identity of women is entirely scripted by these narratives.

Alice Rossi, the well-known sociologist and feminist leader, appears to have realized this to be the case over twenty years ago. After conducting a study on sexual differences, Rossi decided that the supporters of "cultural determinism had got themselves into an untenable position. Instead of replacing outdated biological theories with new, accurate knowledge, they are forced to deny that there are any physiological differences between men and women."[49] The new knowledge we will now confront is what neuroscience has to say about sex-specific differences in the human brain.

CHAPTER 3

The Mind Is Its Own Place: Brain Sex

We are evidently unique in our symbolic ability, and we are certainly unique in our modest ability to control the conditions of our existence by using these symbols. Our ability to represent and simulate reality implies that we can approximate the order of existence and bring it to serve human purposes.

—HEINZ PAGELS
The Dreams of Reason

Although life for our hunter-gatherer ancestors seems simple and crude, the picture becomes more subtle and complex when we examine the terms for survival. The male hunter moved warily in small groups through a landscape inhabited by more powerful predators looking for abandoned carcasses, small prey, and better sites for gathering. Hunters relied principally on throwing stones to kill prey, and mutations that enhanced that ability had survival value. Mutations that enhanced the ability to see small objects and to recognize details in a moving environment were similarly advantageous.

While it is wrong to place too much emphasis on aggression as an evolutionary advantageous trait for male hunters, it is equally wrong to ignore it. There is a correlation between higher levels of aggression and the ability to venture forth into the threatening environment of the hunt and successfully kill prey. With the gradual enlargement of the human brain, however, cognitive traits associated with higher brain regions also had survival value.

Hunters who could track prey in unfamiliar territory while avoiding the potentially fatal mistake of getting lost were more likely to succeed in the hunt. Thus mutations enhancing spatial skills, like the ability to image movement in abstract map space and to move from point A to point B in this space, tended to survive in the gene pool. And this was also true of the genes of hunters who could coordinate the activities of the hunt in terms of interdependent roles and patterned behaviors.

While gathering was also a group activity, the traits that provided a survival advantage were not the same. Picture a small group of women, most of whom are carrying children on their hips and picking nuts, berries, and tubers. Success in gathering favored superior hand-eye coordination, and this trait conferred a survival advantage. Gatherers who were better equipped to see in faint light had an advantage because they could gather longer.

Similarly, women with heightened sensitivity to touch, taste, and smell were better able to identify edible foods and to remember where those foods could be found. The terms of survival for gatherers also favored women who could more easily detect the presence of predators with enhanced peripheral vision and sensitivity to loud noises. In contrast with hunting, gathering took place in close proximity to base camp; thus, navigation by familiar objects was more selectively advantageous for women. Other differences in the brains of gatherers and hunters evolved as a result of the alternate characters of their social realities.

Successful child rearing, like gathering, required consensus and cooperation between all adult members of the group. The children of mothers who could live peacefully within the group were more likely to be nurtured by the group and to pass on genes to subsequent generations. Consequently, the ability to read the gestures, postures, and vocal clues that signal emotional states had more survival value for women. An enhanced ability to nurture infants conferred an obvious survival advantage. Nurturant mothers were better able to raise children to child-bearing age and to establish emotional bonds with other mothers. These ancestral women competed, of course, for scarce resource and status, but this competition was within a social context in which the more violent and individualistic competition of the male variety had little survival value.

THE MIRACLE MOLECULE: DNA

The family album containing the record of our hunter-gatherer evolutionary past is DNA, and the legacy of that past begins to unfold following the union of sperm and ovum. Normal females have two long X chromosomes contributed by each biological parent that closely resemble one another. Normal males have a long X chromosome contributed by the mother and a short Y chromosome contributed by the father. Although each sperm and ovum contributes half of the full complement of 46 chromosomes, the ovum provides all of the cytoplasmic DNA.

In normal development, if the wedding of sperm and egg results in an X chromosome from both parents, the fetus will develop as a female. If a Y chromosome from the father is present and a gene known as the sexually determining region on the Y chromosome (SRY) is expressed in about the sixth week of pregnancy, the release of testosterone in the gonads transforms the developing fetus into a male.

The SRY gene accomplishes this feat by interacting with genes that regulate or are regulated by the expression of SRY. The result is a kind of chain reaction in which genes involved in the determination of maleness are activated in a large

number of cells. Until quite recently, it was assumed that a
fetus is basically female and becomes male only if the SRY
gene is expressed. But this assumption no longer holds.
Researchers have discovered a gene on the X chromosome
that seems to play a role in ovarian formation or that serves
as a link between ovary and testes formation.[50]

Since a fetus becomes male as a result of the delicate action
of sex hormones on control and regulatory genes at several
critical points in prenatal development, there is a greater
prospect that something will go wrong. More male than
female fetuses are spontaneously aborted, and males suffer
far more birth defects. Male babies are also plagued by higher
rates of cognitive and behavioral disorders, and are 30 percent more likely to die in the first few months of life.

The rate of cell growth in the human brain following
conception is astonishing, and the population explosion continues outside the womb. The number of neuronal connections in newborns, about 50 trillion, swells to about 1,000
trillion in twelve months. Depending on whether a child
grows up in a rich or an impoverished environment,
neuronal connections can vary by 25 percent or more. As the
brain matures, these cells are organized into roughly forty
different neuronal pathways that coordinate both physical
and cognitive processes. But the result is not precise and
categorically distinct neuronal maps. The hormone-induced
changes are on top of differences associated with unique
genetic inheritance, the levels of hormones vary across individual brains, and the response of brain regions to the
presence of hormones is highly variable.

The walnut-shaped mass of an adult human brain weighs
roughly 3 pounds and contains about 100 billion neurons.
Neurons receive signals on branched extensions of their
bodies, called dendrites, and send them along other extensions called axons. While there is an enormous variety of cell
bodies, axons, and dendrites, the mechanisms of information
transfer between neurons are essentially the same. Informa-

tion moving through an axon is coded in weak electrical impulses, called action potentials, which travel at a maximum speed of 100 meters per second. The key aspect of the code is the frequency, or number, of electrical impulses.

When an action potential reaches the end of an axon, it does not simply cross over to a dendrite in a neighboring neuron. A small gap, or synaptic cleft, separates the axon from a synapse on the dendrite. Communication over this gap is mediated by chemical neurotransmitters released from tiny vesicles in the axon terminals, and results are dependent on the action of the neurotransmitters on the membrane of the target dendrite. The membrane of a dendrite in its normal or resting state has a negative charge on its inner surface with respect to its outer surface. A dendrite will remain in this state, which means that it does not fire, unless its membrane becomes more permeable to sodium ions.

A neurotransmitter functions like a molecular key that can unlock a door, or channel, in the membrane of the target dendrite so that sodium ions can enter. If this occurs, the charge between the inner and outer surface of the membrane is normally altered, and the target neuron is depolarized for about 1 millisecond. Depending on inputs from other synapses on the dendrites of the target neuron, another action potential may be generated. (See Figure 3.1.)

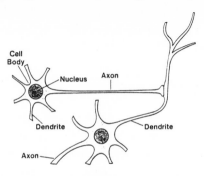

Fig. 3.1

If a neurotransmitter alters the charge of the target neuron so that it is closer to the threshold of the action potential, meaning that it is more likely that an action potential will be generated in the target neuron, it is called excitory. A neurotransmitter that has the reverse effect is inhibitory.

Input from a single synapse does not necessarily cause a target neuron to generate an action potential. A neuron must integrate inputs from as many as 1,000 synaptic impulses to set the frequency of an action potential or to determine whether to create one. In contrast with binary connections or switches, neuronal connections are graded, like a thermostat, and results are highly probabilistic. Predicting with certainty whether the frequency of an action potential will be replicated exactly, increased, reduced, or delayed is virtually impossible.

If we also include in this picture the bewildering variety of neurons and their staggering numbers, it is easy to appreciate why our mental life seems fluid, subtle, and unpredictable. It is trendy these days to refer to the human brain as the "wet machine" or the "biological computer." But these analogies are bogus. Communication within the staggering complexity of neurons in a human brain is very different from that of digital computers, and neuronal patterns are not software programs that rigorously legislate over thoughts and behaviors. Linear and causal models have no place in a discussion of differences in male and female brains, and attempts to predict with certainty how these differences correlate with behavior are futile.

MAPPING THE THREE-POUND UNIVERSE

The first indication following conception that our evolutionary past is present is the manner in which neurons organize themselves into various brain regions. The human brain is an archeological site with the deepest levels consisting of the most ancient structures and the outer layers of the more recently evolved structures. (See Figure 3.2.) Our shared evolutionary history with the reptiles is evident in the brain region that sits above the spinal chord, which consists of structures called the medulla, cerebellum and pons. The medulla controls breathing, heart rate, and digestion, the cerebellum coordinates sense and muscle movements, and the pons manages relays for breathing, hearing, feeding, movement, and facial expression.

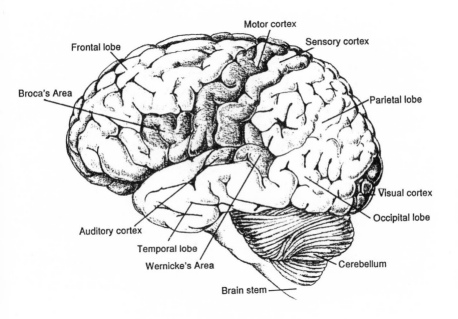

Fig. 3.2. The Human Brain

The next most recently evolved region, essentially alike in all mammals, is the source of emotions. The limbic system sits above the brain stem and under the cortex, and has a number of interconnected structures. (See Figure 3.3, next page.) The thalamus dominates the region above the brain stem and directs all information from the senses to the cortex through various extensions. The lateral geniculate nucleus channels neural input from the retina to visual areas, the medial geniculate nucleus communicates signals from the ears to auditory regions, and so on. The massa intermedia, a band of tissue that connects the right and left halves of the thalamus, has been found to be significantly larger in women than in men. Although male brains are typically more massive than those of females, the massa intermedia in female brains is roughly 53 percent larger.[51]

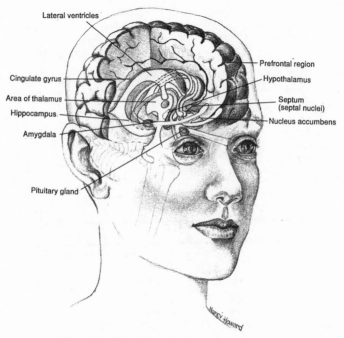

Fig. 3.3. The Human Limbic System

The amygdala, a walnut shaped structure lying deep in the lateral brain, triggers aggressive behaviors, fearful reactions, and positive associations. The hippocampus, which sits adjacent to the amygdala, integrates incoming information as part of the dynamics of long-term memory and makes and stores spatial maps. Since a lab animal whose hippocampus has been destroyed returns monotonously to areas of the cage already explored, this brain region is also associated with the search for novelty. People who have suffered damage to both the amygdala and the hippocampus typically experience global retrograde amnesia and are unable to assimilate new information.

Encircling the hippocampus and other structures of the limbic system is the cingulate gyrus, which connects to a two-way fiber called the fornix. One structure that receives input from the fornix through the hippocampus, the septum, is associated with intense pleasure, such as orgasm. Patients whose brains were implanted with electrodes that allowed them to self-stimulate their septum did so with alarming enthusiasm and were blissfully unconcerned about anything else.

The small but potent hypothalamus is connected to the hippocampus through the fornix and directs most of the physiological changes that accompany strong emotion. Blood pressure, sleep-wake cycles, body temperature, and feeding and drinking are regulated by this brain region. One portion of the hypothalamus, the sexually dimorphic nucleus (SDN), is associated with the sexual behavior of males and females, with neural control of the endocrine glands, and, in human beings, with sexual orientation and gender identity. When a male child is two to four years old, the release of testosterone promotes cell growth and prevents programmed cell death in the SDN. As a result, the SDN of male children roughly doubles in size.[52]

Another portion of the hypothalamus, the medial preoptic area, contains one region that is larger in males than in females and plays a large role in typical male heterosexual copulatory behavior. Some evidence also suggests that damage to this area in male brains results in increased sexual behaviors associated with females.[53] The corresponding region for female sexual behavior in the hypothalamus, the ventromedial nucleus, is associated with sexually receptive behaviors and copulation.[54]

Sex-specific differences have also been found in a region of the hypothalamus called the suprachiasmatic nucleus (SCN). The SCN is involved in the regulation of circadium rhythms, such as the sleep-wake cycle, and longer periodic processes, such as the ovulation cycle. While the volume and cell number in the SCN are roughly the same in men and women, it is more elongated in females and more spherical in males.[55] But more is involved here than anatomical sex-specific brain differences that condition sexual orientation, cyclic biological processes, and copulatory behaviors.

THE WONDROUS NEOCORTEX

The neocortex looks like a redundantly folded sheet and contains 70 percent of the neurons in the central nervous system. It is divided into two hemispheres that process different kinds of information fairly independently, and each communicates with the other via a 200 million-fiber network called the corpus callosum. While the symmetry is not exact, structures in one hemisphere are mirrored on the other. Thus we have two parietal lobes, two occipital lobes, and so on.

The occipital lobes, located toward the back of the head, are associated with the prime visual areas. The temporal lobes, positioned above the ear, are intimately connected with the limbic system that lies below, and are a primary auditory area. Visual messages processed through the occipital lobe also feed back to the temporal lobe. The parietal lobes arch over the brain from ear to ear and contain a schematic map of the body, or a topographic map for motor and tactile responses. (See Figure 3.4, facing page.) The two frontal lobes, located behind the forehead, are control centers that "decide" which responses to make based on feedback from the other brain regions.

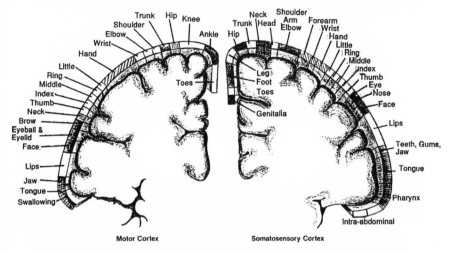

Fig. 3.4

In people with normal hemispheric dominance, the left hemisphere has executive control. This hemisphere manages linguistic analysis and expression, and sequential motor responses or body movements. The right hemisphere is responsible for perception of spatial relationships, faces, emotional stimuli, and prosody (vocal intonations that modify the literal meaning of a word).[56] The two frontal lobes of each hemisphere, located behind the forehead, integrate inputs from other brain regions and are closely associated with conscious decision making. This portion of our brain, which occupies 29 percent of the cortex, has undergone the most recent evolutionary expansion.

The brain processes language by means of at least three interacting neural systems. Nonlanguage interactions between the body and the environment are communicated through sensory and motor systems to neural systems in the left and right cerebral hemispheres. These systems first categorize the information in terms of sequence, shape, color, and emotional states. They then create symbolic representations that are the basis for abstraction and metaphor.

A second set of neural systems in the dominant hemi-sphere generates phonemes, combinations of phonemes, and syntactic rules for arranging words. These systems assemble spoken and written sentences, and perform the initial processing of auditory or visual language signals. A third set of neural systems in the dominant hemisphere mediates between the other two systems, and either translates con-cepts into word forms or words into corresponding con-cepts.[57]

BRAIN SEX IN THE NEOCORTEX

One piece of evidence indicating that the brains of women and men tend to process information differently involves the corpus callosum, or the network of fibers connecting the two hemispheres. A subregion of this network, the splenium, is significantly larger in women than in men and more bulbous in shape.[58] More connections between the hemispheres in female brains could be a partial explanation for another significant discovery—both hemispheres are normally more active in the brains of females.

Computer-based imaging systems, such as positron emis-sion tomography (PET) and magnetic resonance imaging (MRI), allow scientists to assess which areas of the brains of conscious subjects are active. All of these systems use ad-vanced computers to construct three-dimensional images of brains as they process various kinds of information.

In the PET procedure, a simple compound, such as water, is labeled with a radioactive isotope and injected into the bloodstream of the subject. After the radioactive isotope enters the brain, information supplied by the decay of the isotope is recorded by an array of detectors around the head of the subject. When the radioactive isotope decays, positrons, or positively charged electrons, collide with nega-tively charged electrons in the surrounding tissue. The col-lisions create two gamma rays that exit the brain at 180 degree angles. Since there is increased blood flow and metabolism in areas of the brain that are firing more neurons, higher concentrations of gamma rays are detected in these areas. When the information from the detectors is fed into an advanced computer, a metabolic map of the subject's brain is constructed.

Although hundreds of studies on brain-damaged patients have shown that cognitive tasks are more widely distributed throughout both hemispheres in female brains, it could not be said with certainty that the same applied to normal subjects. But over the last decade studies based on PET technology have revealed that cognitive tasks in the female brain tend to be localized in both hemispheres,[59] and that the same tasks in the male brain tend to be localized in one hemisphere.[60]

These studies have not been regarded as conclusive owing to two limitations of PET technology that have contributed to disparate or ambiguous results.[61] The spatial and temporal resolution on PET scans is not sufficiently high to detect small differences in deep brain structures. Also, the procedure can only detect those brain regions that are more active, and does not allow specific brain structures to be targeted and compared. Over the past few years, however, a new imaging system has been developed that overcomes these limitations.

In functional MRI, transitions between the spin of atomic nuclei and certain isotopes of common elements are induced by a specific radio frequency in a magnetic field. The transitions emit a radio frequency signal that is measured by magnetic induction in a receiver coil that is pulsed along three axes to spatially encode the signal. After the signal is stored in a computer with large data storing capacity and graphics capability, three-dimensional displays of slices of specific brain regions are generated. More recently, functional images with very high resolution have been obtained by increasing the number of radio frequencies emitted per unit of time and by using more sophisticated computer hardware and software.[62]

This technology was used in the now famous study at the Yale University School of Medicine on differences between the functional organization of the brains of men and women in the use of language. Thirty-eight right-handed subjects, nineteen males and nineteen females, were shown visual questions and asked to determine whether items were the same or different in four areas—line judgment, letter case, rhyme, and semantic category. The results showed that the male brain performs these tasks in an area known as the inferior frontal gyrus of the dominant hemisphere and that the female brain performs these tasks in the inferior frontal gyrus in both hemispheres.

When those who published this study said that the results of previous studies were "inconclusive,"[63] they were not suggesting, as the press reports alleged, that they were the first to uncover evidence of this kind. They were simply indicating that all subsequent research based on such high-resolution imaging systems should lead to the same conclusions. This also explains why the researchers had no qualms about claiming that their findings were "conclusive" in spite of the small size of the research sample.

In another recent study at the University of Pennsylvania School of Medicine, PET scans were used in combination with high-resolution MRI technology to image the metabolic activity of the brains of thirty-seven young men and twenty-four young women when they were at rest, or not consciously thinking about anything. The study found seventeen brain regions in which there were significant sex differences. It also disclosed that men, on average, have higher levels of activity in the temporal limbic system, a primitive brain region associated with action, while women, on average, have more activity in middle and posterior cingulate gyrus, a more recently evolved region associated with symbolic action. One of the authors of this study explained the distinction as follows: "If a dog is angry and jumps and bites, that's an action. If he is angry and bares his fangs and growls, that's more symbolic."[64]

Here, as in virtually all studies of this kind, the overlap in the brain functions of men and women is enormous. Some of the subjects (thirteen men and four women) had scores that were opposite to the sex-specific indices, and the background of similarities in the profile of metabolic activity was enormous. As the researchers noted, "The similarity attests to the overall reliability of the metabolic parameters and also reminds us that the two cerebral hemispheres in the brains of men and women are fundamentally more similar than different."[65]

LINGUISTIC SKILLS
AND MATHEMATICAL ABILITIES

Neuroscientists speculate that the on-average superior linguistic ability of females results, in part at least, from higher concentration of left brain linguistic functions and more reliance on the right hemisphere. In studies of "mean length utterance," or the average number of words used in sentences, girls have a significant advantage and make fewer mistakes than boys. The higher concentration of linguistic functions may also account for the superior ability of females to learn complex grammatical constructions. This could also explain why girls in elementary and junior high school tend to outperform boys in spelling, capitalization, punctuation, and comprehension of both spoken and written language.[66]

More interaction with the right hemisphere in female brains, which would enhance the range and complexity of linguistic representations, could also contribute to the large sex difference in "associational fluency." One measure of this ability is the number of synonyms that can be generated in a unit of time. In a study of college students, women averaged four synonyms per minute, while men averaged only one and one quarter—or less than half the number for women.[67]

The male disadvantage had nothing to do with vocabulary size; numerous studies have shown that the vocabularies of men and women are virtually the same. It is simply that males on average seem less adept at uncovering subtle nuances and connections in the meanings of words. Women on average are also dramatically better than men in "expressional fluency," or in generating sentences that illustrate grammatical rules. Women also tend to excel in "word fluency"—the ability to think of words that begin with a particular letter.[68]

Sex-specific differences in the left hemisphere have also been uncovered in brain damaged patients suffering from apraxia, or difficulty in selecting hand movements.[69] In one extensive study, 71 percent of women and 7 percent of men who had suffered damage in the anterior left hemisphere had difficulty imitating a simple series of hand and arm movements. When the damage was in the posterior region, the pattern was reversed—12 percent of women and 44 percent of men were impaired.

This research seems to provide partial answers to two large questions. Why are women more skilled in hand-eye coordination and precise hand movements, and why are men more skilled in throwing projectiles and hitting moving targets? The anterior portion of the left hemisphere, where linguistic functions in female brains are more concentrated, is in close proximity of the motor cortex, or the area of the brain that coordinates hand movements. And the posterior portion of the brain, where linguistic functions in males are more densely clustered, lies in closer proximity to both the visual cortex and the brain regions that coordinate limb and muscle movements.[70]

The sex-specific human brain also explains why males on average have a slight advantage, on average, in studying higher mathematics. People who are skilled in mathematics have the ability to image and manipulate symbols and quantities in abstract space, and can do so without appeal to linguistic representations or narratives. The superior linguistic abilities of girls serve them well in dealing with mathematical problems that require verbal reasoning. On average, they perform much better than boys in solving this kind of problem. When the study of mathematics is no longer anchored in verbal reasoning, however, the average performance of boys is better than that of girls.

When we consider that abstract spatial ability is a right-hemisphere function, discrepancies between males and females in the study of mathematics begin to make scientific sense. Since the two hemispheres operate more independently in the male brain, the right hemisphere may be able to solve abstract mathematical problems in a more dedicated fashion with less distracting inputs from the right hemisphere. In any event, the behavioral consequences of this gender-specific difference extend well beyond the study of mathematics.

In an attempt to assess how men and women become familiar with a new place, a psychologist constructed a computer maze in which subjects move down hallways and corridors, turn right or left, and reverse direction by pressing computer keys. In the first phase of the experiment, the maze included landmarks, or points of reference, in the form of letters marking intersections. After the subjects made six practice runs from start to finish, males and females performed about equally well on a timed test. When the landmarks were removed, or the dimensions of the maze changed, the difference was striking. Women found it very difficult to move through the maze in the absence of landmarks, while men seemed not to notice they were missing. The performance of the males was the same without the landmarks.

When the dimensions were changed, the time that the men needed to navigate the maze was much longer, while that of the women was unaffected. What this study, and many others like it, indicates is that men and women tend to construct three-dimensional space differently. The sex-specific female brain is more inclined to rely on narratives featuring visual markers, while that of males favors vectors marking distance and direction from point to point. Thus, removing the landmarks handicapped women, and changing the dimensions handicapped men.[71]

Numerous studies have demonstrated similar correlations between gender-specific cognitive abilities in North America and Western Europe. But we have only recently begun to study correlations between Western and non-Western cultures. In the most extensive and carefully designed study of this kind, high school students in the United States and Japan were administered a battery of tests. Males in both countries outscored females on mental rotations, and females outscored males on word fluency and story recall or comprehension.

The cultural variables surfaced in overall performance by students in each country. Japanese students, who are pressured to take school work more seriously, consistently scored higher than American students in all categories. On the mental rotation test, Japanese girls did better on average than American boys. Yet the nature part of the equation was not missing in the results— the patterns of gender differences in each culture were very similar.[72]

Those who argue that nature has nothing to do with the study of language and mathematics frequently point to some ambiguous results in gender-based studies of the dreaded Scholastic Aptitude Test. While males score 30 to 35 percent higher on average than females on the mathematical section and the ratio of males to females on scores above 700 is thirteen to one, there are no significant gender differences in scores on the verbal section. This is true in spite of the fact that the test is designed to minimize gender-specific cognitive differences. Why, then, is the male advantage in mathematics so pronounced when the female advantage in language skills is nowhere to be seen?

All that is required to answer this question is a brief review of the verbal part of the exam. One fourth of the questions asked in the "verbal analogies" section have little or nothing to do with linguistic abilities per se. The questions are laid out in a gridlike matrix and require a kind of algebraic analysis of similarities between the meanings of fairly common words in word pairs—A is to B as B is to C and so on. What is being tested here is right brain spatial ability and not left brain language skills. Aware of the problem, the Educational Testing Service included a writing sample in 1995.[73]

More global differences in cognitive and emotional styles can also be attributed in part to the sex-specific human brain. The superior linguistic abilities of women, particularly associational fluency, coupled with more symmetry in hemispheric functions, could explain why women tend to be better intuitional thinkers. If linguistically constructed reality in the brains of women is more richly configured and interconnected, it should follow that women on average are more attuned to nuances, hidden meanings, and associations than men. Womens' greater sensitivity to all aspects of the human sensorium should enhance awareness of subtle perceptual clues and memories of other situations where those clues are present.

In the male brain, the more independent functioning of the left hemispheres probably makes linguistic constructions of reality more factual, linear, and goal directed. Less feedback from the right hemisphere may contribute to reduced awareness of coded meanings in spatial relationships, emotional stimuli, and vocal intonations. If the analysis of a problem or situation invokes the right hemisphere, the more independent functioning of this hemisphere may tend to make the analysis more abstract and geometric. When the male brain makes associations with other similar problems or situations, the bases for these associations are probably similar to the terms of their original construction.

BRAIN SEX AND THE HUMAN SENSORIUM

Selectively advantageous traits of hunters and gatherers also live on in the human sensorium. Numerous studies have shown that women are more sensitive to being touched on all parts of their bodies than men, and women are far more sensitive to being touched on the arms, legs and trunk.[74] Similarly, women have a greater ability to detect faint odors than men, and women are also better at identifying the source of odors. Among men and women in their twenties, females perform on taste tests only slightly better than males. But after sixty-five, male performance drops precipitously, while that of females is only slightly less than it was in their twenties.[75]

Women can also detect lower concentrations of sweet, sour, bitter, and salty tastes, and display different preferences than men in the choice of food. Females on average give the highest ratings to foods with a sucrose level of 10 percent, while males prefer foods with a level of about 20 percent. Small boys typically enjoy foods with sucrose levels at 40 percent while girls in the same age group describe such foods as "much too sweet."[76]

With regard to sight, the picture is a bit more complex. Men on-average are more sensitive to bright lights, while women are better at picking out objects in a dark room. Since the eyes of women also adjust more quickly to shade or dark and are capable of holding an after-image longer, they have an advantage in night vision. Men on-average have more visual acuity, or the ability to see small objects and to pick out moving objects, and sharper vision in the middle of a visual field. But women have superior peripheral vision and outperform men in extracting details from drawings and strings of letters or numbers.[77]

As for sound, women can detect high-pitched sounds better than men, and are far more sensitive to loud sounds. In studies on both children and adults, males could tolerate seven or eight more decibels at every frequency than females. The difference here is not marginal. Since seven or eight decibels is almost twice as loud, males apparently prefer volume levels that are much higher than those preferred by females. If this sex-specific tolerance for loud sounds is learned, it should vary among different age groups. However, given that there is no such variation, it appears to be innate.[78]

BOYS, GIRLS, AND THE S/HE BRAIN

Although some sex-specific behaviors are associated with the action of hormones on the human brain during puberty, the legacy of our evolutionary past is also obvious in infancy and childhood. Infant males are more interested in objects than people and tend to be more physically active. Boys are more skilled than girls in throwing projectiles and at following objects moving in space. Higher levels of aggression in males of all ages have been found to exist in cultures as diverse as those of Kenya, Mexico, India, the Philippines, and the United States.[79] In all of these cultures boys chase, grab, wrestle, favor contact sports, and establish hierarchies based on physical prowess.[80]

Infant females are far more intrigued than infant males by the faces of people and the sounds of their voices. Girls are better than boys at assessing mood based on tones of voice and visual clues, and are more interested in new people than new toys. The games girls play favor cooperation over competition and physical proximity over distance. These games also tend to be based on "single role play"—all the players do the same thing.

Girls at play are more inclined to focus on interactions with other girls and to remain closer to the center of play.

They typically make an effort to assimilate a new member into the play group, and they are more empathetic when a member is in physical or emotional distress. When older girls play with younger girls, they normally compensate for different interests and skill levels by playing at the level of younger girls.[81]

Boys at play are far more likely than girls to explore spaces around objects and to move away from the center of play. The games played by boys are more competitive, more action oriented, and more time consuming. They also feature complex rules, multiple roles, and "player interdependence" —the action of one player affects the next player. While older boys normally allow younger boys to participate, the younger boys are obliged to compete on the same terms and receive minimal attention until they are successful in this competition. Boys also prefer games that allow winners to be clearly differentiated from losers, or those with specific goals, like scoring points.[82]

DEALING WITH DIFFERENCE

The use of qualifiers such as "on-average," "tends," "may," "probably," and "might" in the description of behavior associated with the sex-specific human brain is not a concession to political correctness. It is the only way to characterize such differences. Since the brain of any single individual is unique even on the gross anatomical level, making categorical distinctions between the emotional and cognitive processes of men and women is simply not possible. In virtually all computer-based studies on the mental abilities of men and women, what is most significant is the amazing degree of overlap.

On the other hand, the sex-specific differences that inform these processes result in behavioral tendencies that on average correlate with statistically significant discrepancies in behavior on the group level. These discrepancies force us to conclude that the construction of gender identity in a symbolic universe involves something more than learning gender-specific roles and behaviors. At every stage in the learning process, information foundational to gender identity is processed by and encoded in sex-specific brains.

The aspect of our lives in which the failure to recognize and deal with sex-specific differences in the s/he brain creates the most tension, anxiety, and conflict is in long-term love relationships. If there is to be peace in the American gender war, the negotiations must start between men and women who have been victimized by the demands of modern love. Many of our expectations in dating, courtship, and marriage are not in accord with biological reality. This explains why much of our confusion in the garden of love can be traced to erroneous assumptions about the relationship between sex and gender legitimated by the sex/gender system.

CHAPTER 4

All You Need Is Love?
The S/he Brain and
the Mating Game

The meeting of two personalities is like the contact of two chemical substances; if there is any reaction, both are transformed.

—CARL JUNG

When the research on neurotransmitters associated with being in love first became news, media pundits proclaimed that the grand passions and exalted confusion of romantic love are "caused" by natural love potions in the human brain. Some pundits even envisioned a pill that would either create or eliminate this altered state. The claim that romantic love can be explained by the action of a special class of neurotransmitters is utter nonsense. But it is theoretically possible, however disastrous the consequences might be, to develop the pills.

Mind- or mood-altering drugs have molecular structures that resemble those of neurotransmitters. For example, cocaine resembles dopamine, acts on the dopamine receptors, and tricks the brain into operating as if enormously high levels of this neurotransmitter were present. Similarly, valium reduces anxiety by augmenting the effects of GABA, and Prozac alleviates depression by enhancing the action of serotonin.

Given the destructive influence of artificial substances that induce altered states, why did mutations that produce these states survive in the gene pool? The answer is that the powerful neurotransmitters associated with being in love enhanced the prospect of mating and of successfully rearing children. As anyone who has been in love knows first hand, these love potions propel us well out of the range of normative emotional responses.

Studies of the initial stages of "being in love" indicate that the love object typically becomes the center of the individual's universe, and that even the most mundane and trivial characteristics of the magical other are a source of utter fascination. A large number of respondents in one study said that their thoughts and feelings were fixated on the love object from 85 to almost 100 percent of the time. In the presence of the love object, both men and women said they trembled, felt flushed, stammered, and feared losing control over basic faculties and skills. There was also common agreement about the primary reward for this confusion—95 percent of the males and 91 percent of the females indicated that the best thing about being in love was sex.[83]

The principal neurotransmitter contributing to these behaviors is an excitant amine called phenylethylamine, or PEA. This endogenous amphetamine, or speed, saturates the brain when we fall in love and generates feelings of elation and euphoria. When lovers are giddy, absent-minded, optimistic, gregarious, wonderfully alive, and full of extraordinary energy, they are riding a natural high that results from the action of PEA and possibly two other natural amphetamines—dopamine and norepinephrine. A brain flooded with PEA can override the impulse to sleep and allows lovers to dance the night away both figuratively and literally.

The PEA high also appears to be associated with feedback from the amygdala in the limbic system, and this explains why many people feel more erotic when confronted by dangerous situations or the threat of losing a lover. Parachute jumpers were found to have high levels of PEA in their urine before and after jumps, and the levels increased more dramatically in free-fall.[84] In another study, male college students were told to cross one of two bridges—a "fear-arousal" bridge made of board and cable suspended 200 feet above rocks and rapids, and a "control bridge" made of solid cedar built 10 feet above a shallow rivulet. After crossing the bridges, each subject was asked by an attractive female interviewer to fill out a questionnaire scored for sexual imagery. The responses of the group that crossed the fear-arousal bridge contained far more sexual imagery, and members of this group also made many more attempts to contact the female interviewer after the experiment was over.[85] This apparent linkage between fear and sexual interest not only indicates that the PEA high is associated with a range of experiences, it also suggests that the linkage may be enhanced by learning.

People with low levels of PEA are often romance junkies who are literally "addicted to love," but this is an abnormality.[86] The function of the PEA high in evolutionary terms is to promote mating and the transmission of genes to subsequent generations. After this is accomplished, it is not evolutionarily advantageous to remain in an altered state that could threaten survival. This explains why the brains of most people can sustain high levels of PEA for only about two to three years.[87]

It would not be evolutionarily advantageous for parents who must care for children well into the teenage years to terminate their relationship when the PEA high subsides. As this high diminishes, the brain compensates by increasing the levels of morphine-like substances, or endorphins, that create feelings of calm, security, and well-being. This is the biological component in the transition between passional love and companionate love, or between eros as illogical need and obsession and eros as mutual affirmation and acceptance. The discomfort and anxiety felt by those in long-term love relationships when separated from a partner could be due in part to the rapid decrease in endorphin levels.[88]

In a study of divorce statistics in various cultures, anthropologist Helen Fisher found a correlation between the two- to three-year period during which the human brain can sustain the PEA high and the years in a marriage when most couples divorce.[89] In societies as diverse as Finland, Russia, Egypt, South Africa, and Venezuela, divorce generally occurs early in marriage, reaches its peak during the fourth year of marriage, and gradually declines in later years. Although there are variations from the four-year peak in some of these cultures, Fisher believes this is due to the influence of cultural variables.

In Muslim countries, for example, divorce occurs most frequently in the first few months of marriage when the groom's family has the option of returning the daughter to her family if they are not pleased with her. The fact that the Koran exempts a husband from the obligation to pay half of the wedding fee if he dissolves the marriage prior to consummation may also contribute to early divorce in these countries. Fisher believes that cultural variables could also account for variations in the four-year peak in the United States.

During the period from 1960 to 1980, when the divorce rate doubled, the incidence of divorce peaked in and around the second year of marriage. Did this have anything to do with couples living together, or being in some sense married before becoming legally married? Apparently not. Fisher found that while the number of American couples living together tripled in the 1970s, the peak year for divorce between married couples remained the same.

The cultural variables that explain this pattern could be the attitudes of Americans toward marriage. While people in traditional cultures typically marry for economic, social, and political reasons, Americans marry, says Fisher, "to accentuate, balance out, or mask parts of our private lives."[90] If Americans do not feel as pressured to remain married, it should follow that they are more likely to dissolve marital relationships at the point at which the PEA high subsides.

Oxytocin, secreted by the pituitary gland, has also been implicated in the chemistry of love. This chemical stimulates muscle contraction and sensitizes nerves. In women, oxytocin levels soar during childbirth, in the production of breast milk, and while cuddling infants. During sexual intercourse, higher levels of oxytocin enhance cuddling and promote orgasm in both men and women. One study showed an increase of three to four times over normal levels in men during climax, and the increase for women may be even higher.[91]

NEURONAL PATTERNS
AND THINE OWN TRUE LOVE

Neuroscience has also provided some insights into a phenomenon that has long puzzled social scientists—love at first sight. Even though there are a myriad number of potential mates, powerful attraction between prospective lovers is about as rare as it is spontaneous. From across the crowded room, or at the end of the check-out aisle, there suddenly emerges that special smile, face, and body type that is like no other.

This magical moment for males is accompanied by stiffened muscles, increased heart rate, flushed face, and dilated pupils. Signs of love at first sight for females are tingling palms, hardening nipples, quick and shallow breathing, and dilated pupils. Although we may sense in this situation that some cosmic matchmaker is at work, there is another more prosaic explanation.

From infancy to adolescence, the organization of neuronal patterns in our brains is determined in no small part by environmental stimuli. The totality of our experience is encoded in those patterns, and their dynamic interplay constitutes our subjective realities. Within this maze are neuronal patterns associated with members of the opposite sex which constitute a kind of gestalt image that includes physical features, subtle behavioral clues, and powerful emotional inputs. When we encounter a member of the opposite sex toward whom we feel instant sexual attraction, our brains are constructing an image of femaleness or maleness that activates neuronal assemblages corresponding with this gestalt image, or with what are normally called search images.

The search images that most fundamentally condition sexual attraction develop in childhood and derive from interactions with those closest to us in physical and emotional terms. The boy or girl next door can be a source of these images, but the primary source is normally opposite-sex family members. When we consider that these people share half our genes, the well-known fact that we tend to marry people like ourselves begins to make scientific sense.

Efforts to assess resemblances in the physical appearance and behavior of married couples often use an index called the correlation coefficient. Although this is a statistical measure, it can be described in simple numerical terms. Imagine putting a hundred couples in a room and lining up males and females in respect to one characteristic, such as age. If a married couple ends up at the same place in the line, say at number thirty-three, the correspondence is perfect and the correlation coefficient is plus 1. Minus 1 designates a perfect opposite match, as in youngest woman is married to oldest man. If the correlation is random, as in youngest woman is just as likely to be married to a younger as older man, the coefficient is zero.

The highest correlations, typically around plus 0.9, are for age, race, ethnic background, religion, socioeconomic status, and political views. Measures of personality, such as extroversion or introversion, and IQ levels normally fall out at around plus 0.4. This much seems obvious. But what about physical characteristics? Statistically significant correlations have been found between a large number of physical traits that most of us would never imagine had anything to do with the sources of our sexual attraction.

Correlations of about plus 0.2 have been discovered between length of earlobes, lung volume, circumferences of wrists and ankles, and distance between eyes in married couples from cultures as diverse as Chad and Poland. In some instances, such as the length of middle fingers, the correlation is an astonishing plus 0.61.[92] The best explanation for these results is that the gestalt image that informs our attraction to members of the opposite sex is constituted by images of those who share half our genes—opposite-sex members of our family.

THE NONVERBAL LANGUAGE OF LOVE

The nonverbal language of love also attests to the legacy of mate selection among our hunter-gatherer ancestors. Women in cultures as diverse as those in Amazonia, Japan, Africa, France, Samoa, and Papua flirt using virtually the same sequence of expressions. These women first display sexual interest by smiling at the potential love object with eyebrows lifted and eyes opened wide. They then drop the eyebrows, tilt their heads down and to the side, and look in another direction.[93]

Given the importance of eye contact in the mating game of hunter-gatherers, the fact that gazing is the most obvious and universal flirtation signal should come as no great surprise. Men and women in all cultures stare intently into the eyes of potential sexual partners for several seconds, and extreme attraction is signaled by dilated pupils. This is followed by an impulse to close the eyelids, drop the gaze and look away. A look back in the direction of the source of this attraction tends to be furtive and is typically accompanied by meaningless gestures that signal anxiety, like fondling objects, fidgeting, and touching hair. [94]

If the physiological responses associated with love at first sight do not prove too disabling and conversation ensues, another indicator that a sexual liaison may be in the offing comes into play. The gestures made by men and women tend to mirror one another, or to become more synchronous. When he lifts his drink and turns his head right, she lifts her drink and turns her head left. When she touches her hair, he touches his hair, and so on.

Increased physical proximity, like leaning forward and positioning arms and legs closer together, is another sign of increased sexual intimacy. The prospect of further intimacy is typically assessed by "casually" touching a wrist, a shoulder, or a forearm. If the party that is touched does not touch in return, or reacts to being touched by moving out of intimate space, this signals reluctance to become more sexually intimate. But if the potential lover mirrors this laying on of hands behavior, a major obstacle on the road to sexual intercourse may have been eliminated. While the sexual mores of some cultures forbid displays of mirroring behaviors, they exist in every society where men and women are free to choose one another as mates.[95]

If we can believe the results of studies of nonverbal sexual interaction, most American cultural narratives that celebrate male sexual prowess are in need of revision. Researchers have found that American women initiate nonverbal flirtation cues, including the critical first touch, over two-thirds of the time. Follow-up interviews with these women revealed that they were very aware that this was the case.[96]

It is also conceivable that the two-thirds percentage is low due to the influence of cultural narratives. Studies of cross-cultural sexual practices confirm that women normally take the initiative in making sexual advances in virtually any society where they are allowed to do so.[97] This lends support to the thesis that face-to-face coitus, concealed ovulation, and orgasm conferred more power on our female ancestors in the choice of mates.

There are also transcultural patterns in wooing or courtship rituals. In all human societies males offer females food and gifts in the hope of winning sexual favors. The food offering might be a fish, beer, or sweets instead of dinner at an overpriced restaurant, and the gifts might be cloth, tobacco, and hand-carved figures instead of cards and flowers. But the nonverbal messages conveyed by these enticements are not terribly dissimilar.

After men and women fall into the mind-altered state of the PEA high, behavioral tendencies are translated into actual behaviors in accordance with the rites and rituals of love within particular cultural contexts. The stories, myths, legends, and songs that script these behaviors are clearly not universal. In some cultures, like the Mangaians of Polynesia and the Bem-Bem of the New Guinea highlands, the construct of "being in love" does not even exist.

And yet behaviors associated with this altered state, like suicides of males who are not allowed to marry girlfriends and elopements of star-crossed couples, are not uncommon in these cultures. In addition, according to one recent anthropological survey, multiple aspects of romantic love as it is conceived in the West exist in 87 percent of 168 very diverse cultures.[98]

TO THINE OWN LOVE BE TRUE

Biological factors also condition the form of the institution of marriage. Although 5 to 10 percent of men have several

wives in societies where polygyny is permitted and .5 percent of all women have several husbands in societies where
polyandry is permitted, human society is overwhelmingly
monogamous.[99] The sociobiological explanation for the
prevalence of monandry, or one spouse at a time, is that it is
the most effective strategy for perpetuating genes in offspring. Since male hunter-gatherers did not know when a
female was in estrus, frequent copulation with many females
would be less likely to result in pregnancy. Females in these
tribes could give birth to no more than five children, and so
it was not efficient or practical to mate on a regular basis with
more than one male.

There is, however, a more reasonable explanation why the
human species is overwhelmingly monogamous. Face-to-
face coitus, concealed ovulation, and female orgasm enhanced the emotional bonds between parents and the
prospect of successfully raising dependent children well into
their teenage years. Evolution also provides a partial explanation for higher promiscuity in males. The loss of estrus
in ancestral females resulted in a high frequency of copulation and greater promiscuity among both males and females.

It is also no great mystery why ancestral women would
tend to be less promiscuous on average than men. They were
pregnant for extended periods of time, burdened with the
care of infants and older children, and forced to contend, as
the female hymen attests, with jealous and possessive mates.
In the absence of these constraints, males were able to satisfy
their desire for frequent copulation more easily, and this trait
was perpetuated in the gene pool.

The assumption that males are by nature the promiscuous
sex disguises a more fundamental truth—promiscuity is one
of the prime characteristics of both sexes. In societies where
there is no double standard for adultery, women engage in
this behavior as eagerly as men, even though both suffer from
jealousy.[100] Women commit adultery in all societies where it
is forbidden and harshly punished, and even manage to do

so in some instances with great regularity.[101] This does not mean, of course, that evolution sanctions adultery, but it does implode many of our cultural myths about male sexual prowess.

THE POWER OF LOVE

According to the lyrics of popular music and the plots of movies, television sitcoms, and romance novels, eros not only has the power to save or damn, but can also make us feel blissfully a part of, or terribly alienated from, a meaningful whole. If eros did, in fact, consistently confer bliss on the faithful as a reward for blind devotion, we would probably prohibit by law all scientific research in this sacred domain. As most of its devotees know all too well, however, this deity has a Janus face.

One indicator of the troubled state of eros in this culture is that contemporary teenagers are much more likely to become sexually involved at an early age. Among ninth graders, 48.7 percent of males and 31.9 percent of females have had sexual intercourse. The percentage of sexually active teens grows steadily through the tenth and eleventh grades, and reaches 76.3 percent of males and 66.6 percent of females in the twelfth grade.[102]

Studies also show that the vast majority of these young people do not habitually use contraceptives or take other steps to avoid sexually transmitted disease. About 2.5 million U.S. teenagers contract a sexually transmitted disease every year, meaning one in four sexually active adolescents is infected. While there are no reliable figures on unwanted pregnancies and abortions, both appear to be at record-breaking levels.

Recent studies have also indicated that large numbers of American teenagers are involved in physically abusive dating relationships. It is estimated that 25 percent of female teenagers experience physical violence in dating relationships, and the figure is probably higher in urban school systems.[103] What most alarms school counselors is that the female victims normally attempt to remain in these relationships, do not disclose to parents or other adults that they are being physically abused, and typically refuse to press charges even after being hospitalized due to injuries. Adolescent females who have been asked about this behavior typically reveal that they perceive physical abuse by their boyfriends as an act of love.

A less appalling but no less important indicator of the sorry state of eros in this culture is the incidence of divorce and the emotional trauma that normally results. Even though the divorce rate declined marginally in the United States during the 1990s, it is still estimated that 50 percent of marriages will end in divorce. The vast majority of those who live through the aftermath of a failed marriage will, in a remarkable display of the triumph of hope over circumstance, remarry within a few years.[104] Forcing people to remain in unworkable and unsatisfactory marriages is not the solution. Yet most divorced people do not have a clear understanding of why the marriage was unworkable or unsatisfactory.[105]

In the drama of marital infidelity, Shakespeare's "green-eyed monster that doth mock the meat it feeds on" looms large. Male jealousy in this culture is a leading cause of spousal homicide, and jealousy is one of the primary causes of suicide for both sexes.[106] Based on the evidence, it seems that refusing to consider the ways in which scientific knowledge can heal the body of eros is not unlike refusing to allow science to cure a disease with medication.

LESSONS FROM THE S/HE BRAIN

American popular culture creates the impression that most of us are constantly preparing for, recovering from, or engaging in promiscuous sex. But the results of what may be the first truly scientific survey of American sexual behavior,

The Social Organization of Sexuality, present a very different picture.[107] Based on face-to-face interviews with a random sample of almost 3,500 Americans, ages 18 to 59, researchers found that an average American male has six sexual partners over a lifetime while an average American female has two sexual partners.

Equally significant, adultery appears to be much more the exception than the rule. Nearly 75 percent of married men and 85 percent of married women surveyed said they had never been unfaithful. As for frequency of sexual intercourse, almost 40 percent of married people indicated they had sex twice a week, compared with 25 percent for single people.[108]

Obviously, a host of cultural and personal variables contribute to these behaviors, and the legacy of our evolutionary past does not legislate over them. Nonetheless, this legacy lives on in selectively advantageous behavior that encourages powerful emotional bonding between potential parents—face-to-face coitus, concealed ovulation, private sex, and female orgasm. Hence, the mating game in our species is framed around biological regularities that favor interdependence, cooperation, and long-term involvement.

This does not mean, of course, that evolution is a moral philosopher that dictates the terms of successful love relationships. On the other hand, behavioral tendencies associated with the s/he brain do have something to say about ways in which we might seek to sustain and improve these relationships. Since the human brain cannot sustain the PEA high for more than a few years, the idea that this altered state is a precondition for a healthy love relationship is not in accord with biological reality. Yet we are incessantly bombarded with messages in print and electronic media that the opposite is true.

That the vast majority of those who fall in love and enter long-term relationships elect to have children also makes sense from a biological perspective. The PEA high evolved in our species not only because it facilitated frequent intercourse and impregnation, but also because it encouraged the emotional bonding required to raise big-brained infants to the point at which they could bear offspring.

The fact that the s/he brain generates an increased level of morphine-like endorphins as the PEA high subsides is another lesson of evolution that we should take seriously. The transition from passional love to companionate love, as previous generations seem to have known far better than our own, is natural and necessary, and can signal the beginning of a new and potentially very satisfactory phase in love relationships.

This does not mean that sex between marital partners ceases to play a central and vitally important role in sustaining relationships, or that the excitement of being in love is forever lost. Rather, it suggests that the feelings of calm, security, and well-being occasioned by higher levels of endorphins are probably more conducive to maintaining relationships between responsible adults and raising children.

Evolution also has something to say about the fact that teenagers tend to be more victimized by sexual love than other segments of the population. Since the biological clock of ancestral females ran more slowly than that of contemporary females due to dietary differences, ancestral females reached puberty several years later on average. But since ancestral hunter-gatherers began to mate and reproduce shortly after reaching puberty, all of the mechanisms that facilitate this process are powerfully at work in the lives of teenagers.

Concern about sexually transmitted diseases, particularly AIDS, has resulted in numerous campaigns to promote the use of condoms. Many of these campaigns suggest that virtually all the dangers associated with adolescent sexual behavior can be eliminated by consistent use of condoms. From the perspective of evolution, however, sex is not a form of recreation or a game that can be played with no liabilities on the part of the players.

The biological mechanisms of human sex evolved under special conditions in accordance with the most fundamental compulsion of life—passing on genes to subsequent generations. We have done untold violence to teenagers by failing to make them sufficiently aware of the terrible force of this compulsion, and the enormous difference between sex as a biological reality and sex as it is depicted in popular culture.

It is also likely that the failure to curb teenage pregnancy rates by teaching birth control methods is due to something more than ill-conceived sex education programs. The compulsion to pass on genes to subsequent generations involves brain regions and associated behavior that evolved long before centers of higher cognition in the neocortex. This could partially explain why many teenagers who have been well schooled in birth control methods get pregnant. Even in the tumultuous phase of human sexual life called adolescence, however, learning is empowered to alter behavior, and the lessons of evolution could greatly facilitate the learning process.

That feedback from the amygdala is associated with the PEA high probably accounts for much of the seductive appeal of sex and violence in television programs, films, and popular music. Since this feedback is apparently enhanced by learning, however, this "entertainment" may not be as innocent or innocuous as the decision makers in the sex and violence industry claim. If an individual is repeatedly exposed to visual and auditory stimuli that links sex and violence, the association tends to be encoded in the neuronal organization of his or her brain. If this individual is not sufficiently exposed to healthy displays of sex without violence, it is extremely difficult, as many studies have shown, to eliminate sexually violent behavior.

When battered female adolescents confess that they feel that physical violence in sex is an act of love, the emphasis should be placed on the word "feel." If the neuronal organization of the brains of these young women, as well as that in the young men who abuse them, have encoded a linkage between sex and violence, it is probably feeling, as opposed to a lack of a proper understanding of sexual love, that drives this behavior. If this is the case, we may soon find a means of regulating the sex and violence industry based on something more than the opinions of the "moral majority," or standards for sexual behavior grounded only in religious tradition and moral philosophy.

Knowing the codes of evolution in flirtation behavior and the dating game also has its advantages. Obviously, sexual attraction is powerful, and men and women will not keep scorecards to check out their progress. Because the biological predispositions in the sh/e brain are quite malleable in the learning process, the scorecard approach could do more harm than good. On the other hand, familiarity with the biological codes does provide a larger awareness of the difference between a response that is merely warm or friendly and one that signals sexual attraction.

If women tend to initiate the first touch in flirtation behavior, men should be well aware of this fact, and if women tend to be the decision makers in the initial stages of dating behavior, men should obviously know this as well. The absence of mirroring behavior may or may not signal sexual responsiveness, and the presence of this behavior is not a green light for sexual intimacy. Knowing that this behavior is usual could check sexually inappropriate behavior on the part of both men and women. More important, much of the mythology in this culture about male sexual prowess does not accord with biological reality. Thus, the myths must be revised if we are to make peace in the American gender war.

Research on the s/he brain also has a lot to say about the single greatest source of dissatisfaction in love relationships and the primary reason why women file for divorce—lack of communication and the need for more emotional closeness.

That men and women tend to speak different languages and to live disparate emotional lives is not a mystery beyond understanding. Behavioral tendencies associated with sex-specific differences in the s/he brain condition these behaviors. Understanding the tendencies will not eliminate mystery in love relationships, but understanding that reality as it tends to be constructed in the brains of men and women is both the same and different could help to define the terms for peace in the American gender war.

CHAPTER 5

The Myth of Male Pathology: The S/he Brain in the Kingdom of Eros

Perhaps if equality did not require uniformity, we, as women, could demand it less ambivalently.

—CHRISTINE LITTLETON
California Law Review

Although the love industry does not attribute any differences in the conversation styles of men and women to the sex-specific human brain, there is a growing consensus that it is extremely difficult to eliminate them. One indicator of this change is linguist Deborah Tannen's book *You Just Don't Understand: Women and Men in Conversation.*[109] The premise of this book is that while men use conversation "to preserve their independence and negotiate and maintain status in a hierarchical social order," women use conversation as "a way of establishing connections and negotiating relationships."[110] Based on this assumption, Tannen concludes there are some large differences in the language of men and women.

Men, she says, are more comfortable with public speaking, or "report-talk," and women are more comfortable with private speaking, or "rapport-talk." Men use language that is abstract and categorical, or communicate in "messages," and women use language that conveys subtle nuances and hidden meanings, or communicate in "metamessages." Similarly, men respond to problems with concrete solutions and suggestions, and women respond with empathy and an emphasis on community.

Competitive males, claims Tannen, favor "commands," or statements that indicate what should be done without qualification, while consensus-building females favor "conditional propositions," or statements prefaced with words like "let's," "we could," and "maybe." Whereas males talk about their status in terms of simple descriptions of individual skills and achievements, Tannen claims that females do so with complicated descriptions of overall character.

Obviously, this sparse theoretical framework does not account for the enormous popularity of Tannen's book. What most impresses readers are the conversations that Tannen uses to illustrate the distinctive character of the language used by men and women. The following exchange occurs when a husband indicates that he did not get enough sleep:

HE: I'm really tired. I didn't sleep well last night.
SHE: I didn't sleep well either. I never do.
HE: Why are you trying to belittle me?
SHE: I'm not! I'm just trying to show you I understand!

"This woman," says Tannen, "was not only hurt by her husband's reaction; she was mystified by it. How could he think she was belittling him? By 'belittle me,' he meant 'belittle my experience.' He was filtering her attempts to establish connection through his concern with preserving independence and avoiding being put down."[111]

In a discussion of the differences between messages and metamessages, Tannen quotes from Anne Tyler's novel, *The Accidental Tourist*. At this point in the narrative the character Macon has left his wife and has moved in with a woman named Muriel. The conversation begins when Macon makes an observation about Muriel's son:

"I don't think Alexander's getting a proper education," he said to her one evening.

"Oh, he's okay."

"I asked him to figure what change they'd give back when we bought the milk today, and he didn't have the faintest idea. He didn't even know he'd have to subtract."

"Well, he's only in second grade," Muriel said.

"I think he ought to go to private school."

"Private schools cost money."

"So? I'll pay."

She stopped flipping the bacon and looked over at him. "What are you saying?" she said.

"Pardon?"

"What are you saying, Macon? Are you saying you're committed?"

Muriel then tells Macon that he must decide whether he wants to divorce his wife and marry her, and that she will not put her son in a new school when he could be forced to leave if Macon returns to his wife. Confused and frustrated by Muriel's attack, Macon responds, "But I just want him to learn to subtract." The problem, writes Tanner, is that "Macon is concerned with the message, the simple matter of Alexander's learning math. But Muriel is concerned with the metamessage. What would it say about the relationship if he began paying for her son's education?"[112]

Some reviewers of Tannen's book have rightly complained that these differences are made to appear too categorical, but they also concede, along with the majority of other reviewers, that Tannen has disclosed some actual disparities in the language used by men and women. How, then, does Tannen account for these remarkable differences in the manner in which men and women linguistically construct reality? She appeals to the two-domain distinction sanctioned by the sex/gender system—younger children "learn" these languages from older children in single sex groups on the playground.

BRAIN SEX AND THE WORLD OF WORDS

From our perspective, there is an obvious problem with this explanation—the play behavior that is the alleged basis for learning the different languages is not simply learned. It is conditioned by behavioral tendencies associated with the sex-specific human, and this accounts for similar patterns of play behavior in all cultures. While there is considerable variation in the forms of these games, the underlying behavioral patterns are similar. The connection between this play behavior and the communication styles of men and women can be illustrated by making a minor modification in Tannen's thesis statement. Substitute the word "hunters" for "men" and the word "gatherers" for "women":

Hunters preserved their independence and negotiated and maintained status in a hierarchical social order, and gatherers established connections and negotiated relationships.

This is a fairly apt description of the conditions of survival for single-sex groups of hunter-gatherers. These conditions resulted in the evolution of sex-specific differences in brain regions associated with sensory and motor skills. This legacy from our evolutionary past conditions the single sex-play of children. However, what is the connection between the brain regions associated with this behavior and the languages used by men and women? The development of the more recently evolved brain regions associated with language skills was in concert with and conditioned by previously evolved brain regions associated with sex-specific sensory and motor skills. This contributed to sex-specific differences in linguistic and other cognitive functions in the neocortex.

The two hemispheres of the male brain tend to operate more independently of one another, resulting in fewer inputs from the right hemisphere. Since linguistic constructions of reality are typically more confined to the left hemisphere in the male brain, they are probably more constrained by the linear, categorical and causal cognitive processes of that hemisphere. Assuming that these constructions feature fewer of the cognitive processes associated with the right hemisphere, this should correlate with less awareness of coded meaning in spatial relationships, emotional nuances in behavior, and vocal intonations that alter the literal meanings of words.

When the male brain confronts a problem that invokes right-hemispheric functions, the solution is largely conditioned by the cognitive processes of that hemisphere. Therefore, the solution may tend to be more grounded in the abstract and spatial character of these cognitive processes. When this solution is translated into linguistic representations in the left hemisphere, there should be a higher probability that it will reflect the terms of constructing reality associated with the right hemisphere.

From this perspective, Tannen's commentary on male language makes some scientific sense: report-talk and messages probably reflect the orientation toward action associated with higher reliance on the primitive region of the limbic system in the male brain and with an orientation toward linear movement in abstract map space in the neocortex.

The usual biological explanation for the male tendency to give commands is the male's higher levels of aggression. At the same time, this linguistic habit also seems consistent with the manner in which reality tends to be constructed in the male brain. Commands may reflect the bias toward action and the organization of particulars in terms of movement between points in map space. Men may, therefore, perceive commands, as opposed to requests, as being more consistent with their sense of the real and as a more expedient way to solve problems.

The relationship between the two hemispheres in the female brain tends to be more symmetric, and there is a greater degree of interaction between these hemispheres.

Since linguistic constructions of reality in this brain appear to invoke a wider range of right-brain cognitive functions, this may enhance awareness of emotionally relevant details, visual clues, verbal nuances, and hidden meanings. This awareness could also be enhanced by more extensive connectivity to neuronal patterns that represent associations and memories.

This suggests that the female brain tends to construct linguistic reality in terms of more extensive and interrelated cognitive and emotional contexts. If this is the case, all aspects of experience may appear more interdependent and interconnected, and this could contribute to the tendency to perceive people and events in a complex web of relation. This may explain why the language of women tends to feature a more profound sense of identification with others, or why this language seems more "consensual." From this perspective, rapport-talk may reflect this sense of identification and may satisfy the need to feel interconnected. Metamessages, which allow analysis of single events to be extended through a complex web of relation, also seem consistent with the manner in which the female brain tends to construct reality. Since this reality seems more consensual, women may be more inclined to regard decision making as consensual and to privilege the "us" over the "I." In the female brain, higher reliance on the portion of the limbic system associated with symbolic action could also contribute to these tendencies.

Sex-specific differences in the human sensorium also contribute to discrepancies in the conversational styles of men and women. As a result of their greater sensitivity to touch, taste, and smell and their superior peripheral vision, women probably factor in more refined sensory information into their linguistic constructions. Similarly, men's superior visual acuity and their sharper vision in the middle of the visual field may contribute to the male tendency to perceive reality in terms of individual objects. The male's tendency to construct reality in terms of vectors marking distance and direction in map space could be another reason why the language of men tends to be more abstract and object oriented.

THE SOCIETIES OF MEN AND WOMEN

Brain science is also in the process of dispelling some myths about the single-sex group behaviors of men and women. Numerous studies have shown that men feel close to other men when working or playing side by side while women feel close to other women when talking face to face.[113] Male group behavior is characterized by an emphasis on space, privacy, and autonomy, and female group behavior by a need to feel included, connected, and attached.[114] Male conversation tends to center around activities (sports, politics, work), and personal matters are discussed in terms of strengths and achievements. In contrast, female conversation is more likely to center around feelings and relationships, and to reflect considerably less reluctance to reveal fears and weaknesses.

As mentioned earlier, men and women also appear to experience intimacy in disparate ways. The index of male intimacy is the degree of comfort and relaxation felt with other men when engaged in activities. Even when men comfort one another in crisis situations, such as the loss of a family member or a spouse, it is physical presence, rather than intimate talk, that tends to be most valued. This emphasis on action also characterizes male expressions of intimacy, such as making physical gestures, helping move furniture, and repairing cars.[115]

The index for intimacy among women is the extent to which personal feelings can be shared in a climate of mutual support and trust. What tends to be most valued in these interactions is confirmation of feelings as opposed to constructive criticism and advice. When women are asked to describe the benefits of such conversations, they typically mention relief from anxiety and stress, feeling better, and a more enhanced sense of self-worth. Although women also express intimacy by doing things for other women, the doing is typically viewed as an occasion for verbal intimacy.[116]

The male bias toward action as an expression of intimacy is apparent in male humor. When men joke, tease, and "horse around," this is typically accompanied by physical movements and gestures. In group activities that permit verbal exchanges, this kind of humor, more often than not, is the primary mode of interaction.[117] The response of males to depression also favors action, or a tendency to "run" when overcome with sadness, anxiety, and dread. When men talk about their depression in therapy, they typically "rush through" an account of their emotions and describe depression with action metaphors, such as "running in place," "running wide open," and "pushing the edge."[118]

When women are clinically depressed, they are more willing to talk about their feelings, to find opportunities to do so with other women, and to seek help in talk therapy. Women also typically disclose the sources of depression in detailed narratives that represent and analyze experience. While men often react to clinical depression by running or moving, women favor sedentary activities like uncontrollable crying, staying in bed, and compulsive eating.

ACTION, TALK, AND THE S/HE BRAIN

The sex-specific patterns that lie beneath the diversity of these behaviors reduce to a male orientation toward action and a female orientation toward talking. Why is this the case? Since the male brain tends to construct reality in terms of abstract solutions and sequential movements in map space, men probably perceive action as more commensurate with their sense of the real. If action in the reality of males seems more "actual" than talking, this could explain, in part, why men are more inclined to associate intimacy with shared activities.

Brain science also suggests that male action in response to depression is something more than a learned avoidance strategy. It could be motivated, like the female tendency to engage in compulsive eating, by an irrational impulse to return to a positive emotional state. The same could apply to the tendency of males to describe feelings with action metaphors. If reality as it is constructed in the male brain privileges action over talking, men may sense that action metaphors are more descriptive of their feelings. Since these constructions are probably less infused with feelings, this could explain, in part, why men have more difficulty talking about feelings.

Neuroscience also suggests why women seem to view talking as conveying more emotions than action. If linguistic constructions of reality in the female brain feature a more extended network of perceptions, memories, associations, and feelings, the real could be more closely associated with language. This could also explain why women favor "rapport-talk," or conversations about the personal and the private. If this talk is more commensurate with the actual character of reality in the female brain, women might depend on conversation to reinforce their reality more than men.

More emotional content in female constructions of reality could also explain why women are more inclined to equate talking with feeling, and to view caring actions that are not accompanied by verbal expressions of feeling as less than authentic. If linguistic constructions of reality in the female brain feature a broader range of emotional experience, on average women may have less difficulty disclosing, describing, and contextualizing feelings.

Much of what has been said here about the sex-specific male brain relates to behaviors associated with the response of men to spectator sports like baseball, football, ice hockey, and soccer. Men spend inordinate amounts of time watching these sports on television, and pay out large sums of money to witness the games first hand in uncomfortable seats in overcrowded stadiums and coliseums. When this is a group activity, seemingly uncontrollable urges to release animal-like cheers, groans, and screams are punctuated by talk of strategy, field position, and the success or failure of key players.

A winning season for a favorite team can occasion gleeful camaraderie, and a losing season endless opportunities to commiserate, complain, and look forward to a better tomorrow. Sons often recall bonding with fathers for the first time in ballparks, and these sons often try to recreate this moment with their own sons. Many avid male fans are a walking encyclopedia of sports trivia.

So what can brain science say about a male obsession that many women regard as an unmistakable sign of pathology? Baseball, football, ice hockey, and soccer involve throwing or moving projectiles with the arm, with a stick that functions as an extension of the arm, or with feet and head. The field of competition is a map or a maze, and rules and clearly defined goals are designed to produce winners and losers. Teams have leaders (captains or coaches) who strategize movement in the map space and coordinate the actions of players. The best players have superior speed, visual acuity, and spatial skills.

We have long been accustomed to viewing these games, particularly football and ice hockey, as a competition between warriors on a field of battle where points, as opposed to kill ratios, signal victory. But there is a more sanguine and realistic view. Since these sports mirror the group behaviors of ancestral hunters, they probably allow men to openly identify with behavioral tendencies that condition fundamental aspects of their constructions of reality. Interacting with other men while watching these games could serve to reinforce this reality.

Granted, sanctioning levels of aggression that often result in lifetime injuries or even death seems more than a little barbaric. The primary intent in these games is not, however, to injure or kill. It is to enter into a competition where success is dependent on the ability of members of a group to coordinate movement of bodies and projectiles in spatial dimensions. This could explain why many men derive much enjoyment from discussing game strategy or from engaging in an object-oriented analysis of patterned movements of players in map space.

THE MYTH OF MALE PATHOLOGY

Social scientists have begun to concede that behavioral discrepancies should be recognized and accommodated in relationships between men and women. But since the two-domain distinction sanctioned by the sex/gender system remains firmly in place, the brains of men and women are viewed as gender neutral. When this distinction is wedded to the notion that women are the model for healthy normalcy in love relationships, maleness becomes a condition desperately in need of a cure.

Consider, for example, what social scientists have to say about differences in the languages of men and women. Men are more comfortable giving commands because they are "in charge of making observable changes in the real world," and learn to speak without fear of "giving offense" in "direct, clear, and succinct" fashion. Similarly, the language of women tends to feature conditional statements because women have been obliged in a world dominated by men "to listen more than speak, agree more than confront, be delicate, be indirect, say dangerous things in a way that their impact will be felt after the speaker is out of the range of the hearer's retaliation."[119]

Many social scientists claim that the root narratives in the male language of power can be traced to ancient myths and legends. In one classic myth of the hero, a man ventures forth on a quest, conquers menacing supernatural forces, and returns victorious. What, asks a social psychologist, is the role of women in these narratives? They function as "a snare, an obstacle, a magic power, or a prize."[120]

Another recent study argues that the myth of the hero in male cultural narratives structures autobiographies written by contemporary males. The argument is that this myth entices men to write detailed accounts of their heroic quest to overcome crises, and to depict the women and children in their lives as incidental figures at best. But what is most instructive here for our purposes are the examples of "male" language used to support this thesis.

The following quotation from Lee Iacocca's autobiography is offered as prima facie evidence that he fails to pay proper tribute to a diabetic wife who suffered heart attacks following two crises in his career: "Above all, a person with diabetes has to avoid stress. Unfortunately, with the path I had chosen to follow, this was virtually impossible." Similarly, Chuck Yeager allegedly reveals his inability to appreciate a wife who had four children in rapid succession and was terribly ill during her last pregnancy in this statement: "Whenever Glennis needed me over the years, I was usually off in the wild blue yonder."

Nobel Prize-winner and physicist Richard Feynman receives much the same treatment. While working on the atomic bomb project at Los Alamos, Feynman received word that his wife, who had been ill from tuberculosis for seven years, was dying. After driving home in a borrowed car, Feynman describes what occurred upon his return to Los Alamos: "When I got back (yet another tire went flat on the way), they asked me what happened. 'She's dead. And how's the program going?' They caught on right away that I didn't want to talk about it." We should interpret this statement, says a well known psychologist, as follows: "Was the tire really more important than his wife's death? Unlikely. The point of the narrative of the story: deaths, even of loved ones, are not to interfere with the Quest, the Task, the Goal."[121]

LET US NOT TO THE MARRIAGE OF TRUE MINDS ADMIT IMPEDIMENTS

I do not wish to be too critical of these social scientists. The myth of the hero is an artifact of Western culture that celebrates the power and prowess of men at the expense of women. That Iacocca, Yeager, and Feynman appeal to this myth in framing the narratives of their lives accounts, in part, for their failure to adequately recognize and represent the very real sacrifices of their wives. However, if we factor into this analysis of male language what we know about the sex-specific human brain, these men are clearly not as invidious as they are made to appear.

First, their autobiographies are structured in terms of action and linear movement in map space, and descriptions of places and events are object-oriented. When reasons for undertaking actions are discussed, the analysis is almost invariably abstract. The intent in this analysis is typically to better understand vectors in map space or to assess how decisions frustrated or realized movement toward goals. Similarly, emotions and feelings are relevant in these autobiographies only to the extent that they enhance or retard this movement. While the mania with which these men pursue goals can be attributed to learning, the cognitive traits that inform their narratives are consistent with what we know about the sex-specific male brain.

When Iacocca says, "a person with diabetes has to avoid stress," he is not crudely dismissing his wife's problems or ignoring the sacrifices she made in the marriage. This "message" recognizes that his behavior had a very negative impact on his wife's condition. What, then, does Iacocca's next male "message" convey? "Unfortunately, with the path I had chosen to follow, this was virtually impossible." The operative word is "unfortunately," and it makes apology for choices that made his wife suffer. Also consider Yeager's allegedly heartless comment, "Whenever Glennis needed me over the years, I was usually off in the wild blue yonder." This is a sincere apology for not being available to help and comfort his wife for "years."

The failure to understand nuances in male language is particularly obvious in the commentary on Feynman. The mention of the "flat tire" and the statement, "She's dead. And how's the program going?" function in precisely the way Feynman indicates: "They caught on right away that I didn't want to talk about it." The "they" refers to other men who understand that Feynman's "message" indicates that he has suffered a terrible loss and is in great emotional pain. The perfunctory discussion of the "program" is a "message" that conveys empathy and concern while simultaneously respecting Feynman's wish not to talk openly about the loss.

If we remain attached to the belief that cognitive and behavioral differences between men and women are entirely learned, this will only foster more confusion and conflict in the American gender war. Asking women to compromise the full potential of love relationships because men have learned to be inadequate and are unwilling or unable to behave differently is absurd. It is also absurd to ask men to obviate behavioral tendencies associated with their sex-specific brain.

This point is nicely illustrated in numerous studies of what women expect from men. As we saw earlier, the primary reason why women seek divorce is "lack of communication," or the unwillingness of the ex-husband to talk about or share feelings.[122] At the same time, women regard men who defy the masculine norm by disclosing their fears and emotions as "too feminine" and "poorly adjusted."[123] From our perspective, the expectation that a man must use the language of women without really using this language makes sense. Although women have been repeatedly told that the model for healthy communication in marriage is female, they know from experience that the realities of men and women are not always the same.

Appreciating how men and women tend to construct linguistic reality in their sex-specific brains does not frustrate the desire of women, or men, to communicate better with their partners. In fact, the opposite is true. If discrepancies in these constructions are properly understood, the escalating war of words between men and women might become a thing of the past. The first agreement we should bring to the negotiating table is a willingness to honor and respect the discrepancies.

MAKING PEACE
IN THE AMERICAN GENDER WAR

If this chapter reads like a defense of maleness, that was not the intent. It was to demonstrate that the sex/gender system breeds conflict in the institutional fabric of society at the most basic level—relationships between men and women. If we are to make peace in the American gender war, the terms for this peace must emerge and evolve in interactions between men and women on the individual level. But much more is at stake here than improved communication and understanding between men and women.

In my view, what most imperils this culture is that reality as it tends to be constructed in the sex-specific female brain is conspicuously underrepresented in social, political, and economic reality. This is apparent in the widespread anger, cynicism, greed, and selfishness that sanctions institutionalized poverty, favors corporate interests over human need and environmental impacts, and seeks to deprive women of the right to their own bodies. Women not only belong, as the bumper sticker puts it, in the House and the Senate, they must also find their way into positions of power and influence on every level of society.

The infusion of the total reality into power elites and dominance hierarchies will not occur, however, if women are obliged to compete, think and act like men. They must be able to speak in their individual voices and seek to realize their own visions with the full and certain conviction that this is an inalienable right. What could well be essential to the long-term success of this struggle is an alternative standard for sexual equality based on an improved understanding of the relationship between sex and gender.

Research in neuroscience clearly indicates that the human brain is not a tabula rasa or blank template on which cultural narratives are scripted or imprinted. When men and women learn cultural narratives, they tend to construct these narratives differently owing to innate on-average differences in spatial and linguistic functions, sensory and motor skills, and feedback from the human sensorium. This forces us to draw two conclusions which have enormous consequences for feminist theory: First, since the human brain is sex specific, "male" cultural narratives, or reality as it tends to be constructed in the brains of men, cannot "define" the reality of women. Second, since sameness in the construction of human reality in the brains of men and women is vastly greater than difference, the realities of men and women are not "separate and discrete."

What we know about the sex-specific human brain also challenges the claim that cultural narratives are exclusively male artifacts, or that reality as it is constructed in the female brain is not reflected in these narratives. Granted, the reproductive roles of women conferred a grossly unfair advantage on men in the public domain, and this advantage allowed men to fashion cultural narratives that legitimated their dominance. This does not, however, permit us to conclude, as is often the case in feminist theory, that the only reality reflected in these narratives is exclusively or distinctly male. What it does suggest is that feminists should make profound revisions in the theories and associated methodologies they currently employ in the study of these narratives.

As mentioned earlier, the group that seems to be the best situated to implement an improved standard for sexual equality is the feminist movement, but feminists cannot begin to consider this possibility as long as the sex/gender system remains foundational to feminist theory. In the next chapter, I will attempt to demonstrate that the sex/gender system contributes to the deep divisions and conflicts in the feminist movement, and has also allowed feminists to define the sources of sexual inequality in the American gender war in terms of an endless series of arbitrary differences.

Yet the decision to do so was not taken lightly. Feminist theory has been the source of liberation and empowerment for millions of women, and many of these women are friends and colleagues. If, however, the feminist movement is to remain a political force, it must develop theories that recognize that nature and nurture are interwoven threads in the complex tapestries of our lives. If academic feminists elect to defend the integrity of the sex/gender system, they will forfeit the opportunity to expose sexist abuses of research on the sex-specific human brain. This decision could also put the vast educational enterprise built on this system at risk, and further isolate academic feminists from political realities in the outside world.

CHAPTER 6

Sexual Politics:
The (S x)/Gender System
in Feminist Theory

Resentment is not a wholesome passion. Unlike indignation, it is not an ethical passion. But because it often originates in moral outrage at real injustice, resentment can be made to sound like a commendable passion for social justice.

—CHRISTINA HOFF SOMMERS
Who Stole Feminism?

As we assimilate the political and social implications of research on the sex-specific human brain, we must obviously be prepared to expose those who abuse this knowledge in the service of sexist agendas. The greatest danger, however, is not sexism per se. It is the extrascientific cultural variables that are foundational to our present standard for sexual equality—the two-domain distinction and the law of the excluded middle. Once again, the dire prediction is that if our current standard for sexual equality is not revised, the standard for sameness against which difference is measured will be extended to the sex-specific male brain.

If this assessment is correct, we could be on the verge of a new phase in the struggle for sexual equality in which enormous inequalities could be sanctioned in the name of equality. Yet we cannot hope to obviate this prospect by alleging sexist conspiracies or attacking the validity of scientific knowledge. Apparently, there is only one alternative. Men and women must work together to implement a new and improved standard for sexual equality that is more commensurate with the actual relationship between biological reality and gender identity.

Those who are concerned about sexual equality will be understandably reluctant to abandon the current standard. Differences in biological roles and functions have consistently been used to discriminate against women, and the two-domain distinction obviates appeals to those differences in dealing with gender issues. Since a relationship exists between biological reality and gender identity, however, the distinction not only severs mind from nature and from any sense of intimate connection with biological reality, it also legitimates a standard for sexual equality in which the biological reality of women is virtually erased.

As Catherine MacKinnon puts it, "The sameness/difference approach misses the fact that hierarchy of power produces real as well as fantasized differences that are also inequalities. What is missing is what Aristotle missed in his empiricist notion that equality means treating likes alike and unlikes unlike, and no one has seriously questioned it since."[124] Or as Deborah Rhodes describes the problem, "Women are both the same and different. To determine which side of the sameness/difference dichotomy to emphasize in legal contexts requires some other analytic tool."[125]

If the feminist movement in the academy is to protect and extend the rights and freedoms of women at this critical stage in human history, it must abandon the sex/gender system. Research on the sex-specific human brain clearly indicates that since the human brain is not sex or gender neutral, there is a definite relationship between biological reality and gender identity. Since the two-domain distinction obviates or erases that relationship, the sex/gender opposition is not a true opposition. It functions as a *(s x)/gender opposition* where *(s x)* indicates that biological reality has been erased. This allows gender identity (s x) to be arbitrarily constructed in either-or opposition to male cultural narratives, or *gender=culture* where *gender=male*, and *culture = constructions of reality in male brains*. As a result, the sex/gender system allows the sources of inequality to be arbitrarily defined in the service of particular constituencies and interest groups.

Given that the contributors to this theory number in the tens of thousands, only a representative sample of the best known and most influential theorists are presented here. In addition, space constraints do no permit a description of all the nuances of these theories or all the positions taken by the theorists. The objective is rather to demonstrate that the (s x)/gender opposition is foundational to all of second-wave feminist theory by disclosing its existence in a sufficiently large and diverse sample. It should also be clear that the analysis can be extended to the work of other theorists.

LEARNING FROM (S X)

The anthropologist Sherry Ortner, arguing that the reproductive roles of women are not invested with social status, posits an either-or opposition between women-nature ([s x]/gender) and male-symbolics (gender=culture). She claims that the global dominance of the male symbolic relegates women to a "private zone" where their concrete and associational reality is kept separate from the abstract public lives of men. "We may broadly equate culture," says Ortner, "with the notion of human consciousness, or with the products of human consciousness (i.e., systems of thought and technology), by means of which humanity attempts to assert control over nature."[126] Ortner's solution is to institute massive changes in reproductive and child-rearing practices in order that men can assimilate the heretofore "private zone" of women.

Although Ortner continually refers to woman's special relationship to nature, she contends that the idea that women are closer to nature than men is a cultural product: "Ultimately, it must be stressed again that the whole scheme is a construct of culture rather than a fact of nature. Woman is not 'in reality' any closer to (or further from) nature than man."[127] Since the construct sex is erased in the (s x)/ gender opposition, Ortner can argue that "nature" says nothing "in reality" about gender identity.

Gayle Rubin appeals to psychoanalysis and structural anthropology to posit an either-or opposition between nature-sexuality ([s x]/gender) and culture (gender=culture). Biological reality (s x), she claims, is transformed into the cultural constructs of masculinity and femininity (gender=culture). In Rubin's view, the reproduction of kinship, or the exchange of women, not only sustains male power, but also governs the construction of gender identity via a sex/gender system that relegates women to the domestic sphere and "natural" functions: "As a preliminary definition, a 'sex/gender system' is the set of arrangements by which a society transforms biological sexuality into products of human activity, and in which these transformed sexual needs are satisfied."[128] But since the "sex/gender" system is really a (s x)/gender system, biological reality has nothing to do with gender identity.

Anne Koedt argues that the oppression of women can be traced to the sexual power of men which manifests itself as threatened or actual violence and psychological inducements such as romance. Her hugely popular essay, "The Myth of the Vaginal Orgasm," is credited as providing scientific support for one of the principal arguments of second-wave feminism. Based on Masters and Johnson's laboratory studies of female orgasm, Koedt concluded that it is clitoral, as opposed to vaginal, orgasm, that is essential to a woman's sexual fulfillment: "Although there are many areas for sexual arousal, there is only one area for sexual climax; that area is the clitoris. All orgasms are extensions of sensations from this area."

Since this finding, argues Koedt, destroys the "myth" that women must be penetrated by men to experience orgasm, women can now be sexually independent of men. This, she claims, should cause women to question the meaning of conventional sex and their role in this sex: "Men have orgasms essentially by friction with the vagina, not the clitoral area, which is external and not able to cause friction the way penetration does. Women have thus defined sexuality in terms of what pleases men; our own biology has not been properly analyzed. Instead, we are fed the myth of the liberated women and her vaginal orgasm—an orgasm which in fact does not exist."[129]

Since female clitoral orgasm evolved as a result of mate selection, and since the clitoris can be and often is stimulated to orgasm by the male penis, there is no need to debate the scientific merits of Koedt's arguments. However, we should take note of the role played by the (s x)/gender opposition. It not only allows the connection between female genitalia (sex) and female sexual behavior to be erased (s x), but also erases the connection between intercourse between men and women (s x) and the sexual roles of women (gender). Mary Sherfey is also credited for shoring up the foundations of feminist theory with appeals to scientific truth. The alleged scientific truth is that all human fetuses are "female" during the first weeks of life and remain female if a gene on the X chromosome does not trigger the release of much higher levels of testosterone. This, Sherfey claims, forces us to conclude that women are essentially homosexual and not, as Freud argued, bisexual. While the suggestion that a fetus with male chromosomes is female is a bit farfetched, particularly when there appears to be an equivalent gene for femaleness on the X chromosome, the idea that a fetus in a sexually reproducing species displays a preference toward homosexuality is absurd. Yet the absurd can take on the appearance of the reasonable when the biological reality of the foetus (sex) is erased (s x), and the connection between biological reality (s x) and sexual preference (gender) ceases to exist.

Sherfey also posits an opposition between the female experience of multiple orgasm (s x) and male-defined sexuality (gender=culture). She reinforces this opposition with yet another opposition between biological evolution (s x) and the sexual identity of women (gender): "The nature of female sexuality as here presented makes it clear that, just as the vagina did not evolve for the delivery of big-headed babies, woman's inordinate orgasmic capacity did not evolve for monogamous, sedentary cultures. It is unreasonable to expect that this inordinate sexual capacity could be, even in part, given expression within the confines of our culture."[130] Obviously, evolution (sex) has been erased (s x) in the opposition between the experience of multiple orgasm ([s x] /gender) and male-defined sexuality (gender=culture).

The poet Adrienne Rich sets up an opposition between social institutions that define the reproductive roles and sexual possibilities of women (gender=culture) and the female experience of motherhood ([s x]/gender): "Throughout this book, I try to distinguish between two meanings of motherhood, one superimposed on the other: the potential relationship of any woman to her powers of reproduction and to her children; and the institution, which aims at ensuring that the potential—and all women—shall remain under male control."[131]

Rich's program for undermining the institution and freeing the powers of women from male domination calls for a rebellion against the "present-day patriarchal family with its super-naturalizing penis." It also requires learning from the "erotics" of female masturbation, orgasmic sexual encounters with other women, pregnancy, childbirth, and nursing.[132] Since the biological reality of the female body (sex) is erased (s x), the opposition between erotics ([s x]/

gender) and the cultural identity of women (gender=culture) is merely an opposition. Hence the experience of the female body (s x) can be viewed as a social construction in a culture in which gender identity and sexual behavior are controlled and defined by a male "institution."

Mary Daly posits a ([s x]/gender)/(gender=culture) opposition between "gyn/ecology" and patriarchal anthrocentrism. She claims males sustain dominance in all cultures through sexual violence, and that patriarchy structures all institutions, ranging from religion to medicine to science. Daly urges women to subvert this "phallic" culture by reversing male myths and renouncing male language and beliefs: "The fact is that we live in a profoundly anti-female society, a misogynistic 'civilization' in which men collectively victimize women, attacking us as personifications of their own paranoid fears, as The Enemy. Within this society it is men who rape, who sap women's energy, who deny women economic and political power." The society that will displace this "State of Patriarchal Power Paralysis" lies, says Daly, "beyond the limitations of the label anti-male, it is absolutely Anti-androcat, Amazingly Anti-male, Furiously and Finally Female."[133] Obviously, this entire argument is premised on a ([s x]/gender) /(gender=culture) opposition between gyn/ecology and the male patriarchal culture.

(S X)/GENDER AND THE ETHICS OF CARE

Some feminists maintain that learning from the female body (s x) explains why the ethical reality for women is utterly different from that of men. Sara Riddick argues that the experience of mothering (s x), which she does not limit to biological mothers (s x), allows women to assimilate values and knowledge ([s x]/gender) that provide an ethical alternative to male aggression (gender=culture). This learning experience (s x) results, she claims, in "maternal thinking" ([s x]/gender), which is characterized by reconciliation, a refusal to separate ends from means, and empathy and respect for others.

Riddick's more humane world requires the displacement of male symbolics (gender=culture) by the politics of peace and ecology that flows from the ethics of maternal thought ([s x]/gender): "Briefly my claim is this: the conventional and symbolic association between women and peace has a real basis in maternal thinking. Out of maternal practice a distinctive kind of thinking arises that is incompatible with military strategy but consonant with pacifist commitment to non-violence."[134] Since the (s x)/gender opposition allows the biological experience of the mother (sex) to be erased (s x), maternal thinking is entirely learned.

Nancy Harstock claims that women learn to construct reality by transforming natural substances in activities like cooking, and by the experiences of menstruation, coitus, pregnancy, childbirth, and lactation. These learning experiences, she says, engender "opposition to dualisms of any sort, valuation of concrete, everyday life, sense of a variety of connectednesses and continuities both with other persons and with the natural world. If material life structures consciousness, women's relationally defined existence, bodily experiences of boundary challenges, and activity of transforming both physical objects and human beings must be expected to result in a world view to which dichotomies are foreign."[135]

Since "bodily experiences" (sex) are erased (s x), the resulting (s x)/gender opposition allows "transforming physical objects" (gender) to be conflated with "transforming human beings" in childbirth and child rearing (s x). The (s x)/gender learning experiences of women exist in either-or opposition to that of men (gender=culture), and so men "must" construct reality based on "dichotomies," and women "must" construct reality in the absence of "dichotomies."

Carol Gilligan claims that women learn an "ethics of care" as a result of bonding with mothers ([s x]/gender), while men learn an "ethics of justice" (gender=culture) as a result of separation from mothers: "The moral imperative that emerges repeatedly in interviews with women is an injunction to care, a responsibility to discern and alleviate the 'real and recognizable trouble' of this world. For men, the moral imperative appears rather as an injunction to respect the rights of others and thus to protect from interference the rights to life and self-fulfillment."[136]

The erasure of biological reality in mother-child relationships (s x) allows Gilligan to view the "different voices" of men and women ([s x]/gender) as learned in a male-dominated social reality (gender=culture): "As we have listened for centuries to the voices of men and the theories of development that their experience informs, so we have come more recently to notice not only the silence of women but the difficulty of hearing what they say when they speak. Yet in the different voice of women lies the truth of an ethic of care, the tie between relationship and responsibility, and the origins of aggression in the failure of connection."[137] While Gilligan does not claim that the "different voice" of women is superior to that of men, the (s x)/gender opposition obliges her to view the voices of men and women as quite disparate and distinct.

Dorothy Dinnerstein draws on social psychology to posit a (s x)/gender opposition between the procreative functions of women (s x) and the socially constructed identity of women (gender=culture). "It is senseless," writes Dinnerstein, "to describe our prevailing male-female arrangements as 'natural.' They are of course a part of nature, but if they contribute to the extinction of the species, that fact would be part of nature too. Our impulse to change these arrangements is as natural as they are, and more compatible with our survival on earth." In order to change the arrangements, she continues, "we need to understand not only the societal mechanisms by which they are supported, but the central psychological 'adjustment' of which they are an expression."[138]

With biological reality (sex) erased (s x), Dinnerstein can claim that male-female arrangements are not "natural," even though they are "a part of nature" (s x). In the absence of any linkage between nature (s x) and sexual roles (gender=culture), the "arrangements" can be "changed" by examining the arbitrary "societal mechanisms" that structure them and the "psychological 'adjustment' of which they are an expression" (gender=culture): "So the essential fact that paternal authority, the fact that makes both sexes accept it as a model for the ruling of the world, is that it is under prevailing conditions a sanctuary from female authority."[139]

Dinnerstein's examination of the "arrangements" takes the form of an account of the pre-Oedipal stage in which sex-specific learning experiences ([s x]/gender) encounter paternal authority (gender=culture). Dinnerstein claims that the fear occasioned in male infants by the loss of absolute dependence on the mother manifests itself as a compulsion to control women. She concludes that the unbounded sense of nonself in female infants occasioned by absolute identification with the mother manifests itself in an attraction to control men in a world in which the parameters of "self" are defined by men. In this instance, the (s x)/gender opposition erases biological reality (s x) even in the prelinguistic stage of human development.

Nancy Chodorow maintains that since the sexual division of labor (gender=culture) places the burden of parenting on women (s x), females develop relational capacities by internalizing the roles of mothers ([s x] /gender) while males learn to reject the female aspects of themselves in order to identify with adult males (gender=culture). As a result, says Chodorow, women display the ability to identify with the needs and feelings of others, and men display a defensive desire for autonomy based on the abstract model of the absent father.

"I argue," writes Chodorow, "that the contemporary reproduction of mothering occurs through socially structurally induced psychological processes. . . .The sexual and familial division of labor in which women are more involved in interpersonal, affective relationships than men produces in daughters and sons a division of psychological capacities which leads them to reproduce this sexual and familial division of labor."[140] Since biological reality (sex) is erased (s x), the resulting opposition between reproductive roles (gender=culture) and reproducing "psychological capacities" ([s x]/gender) allows Chodorow to argue that the "division" between the psychological realities of men and women is an arbitrary product of the socialization process.

(S X)/GENDER AND MARXIST FEMINISM

In Marxist feminism, women are viewed as the proletariat, reproduction (s x) is substituted for production, class refers to sexual classes ([s x]/gender)/(gender=culture), and seizure of control of reproduction (s x) involves full restoration to women of ownership of their bodies (s x) and the social institutions of childbearing and rearing (gender=culture). Hence, the goal of the feminist socialist revolution is the elimination of male privilege and all class distinctions associated with sex or genital differences (s x).

Patriarchy (gender=culture) is defined in feminist Marxism as a set of social relations with a material base that features hierarchical relations between men that subjugate and control women. As Heidi Hartman puts it, "If non-ruling-class men are to be free they will have to recognize their co-optation by patriarchal capitalism and relinquish their patriarchal benefits. If women are to be free, they must fight against patriarchal power and capitalist organization of society."[141]

The most interesting aspect of the erasure of biological reality (s x) in Marxist feminism is that it allows oppositions in economic reality to be constructed as (s x)/gender opposi- tions. Hence, the (s x)/gender opposition between men and women becomes the opposition between proletariat and patriarchal capitalism, and a classless society is a society in which the proletariat displaces the patriarchal capitalism. As Hartman states, "We must insist that the society we want to create is a society in which recognition of interdependence is liberation, and nurturance is universal, not an oppressive practice, and in which women do not continue to support the false as well as the concrete freedoms of men."[142]

In the work of figures like Andrea Dworkin, the erasure of biological reality (sex) by the (s x)/gender opposition becomes rather literal: "The ideology of male sexual dominance posits that men are superior to women by virtue of their penises; that physical possession of the female is the natural right of the male; that sex is, in fact, conquest and possession of the female." And this forces us to conclude, says Dworkin, male ideology sanctions that the views "that the use of the female body for sexual or reproductive pur- poses is the natural right of men; that the sexual will of men properly and naturally defines the parameters of a woman's sexual being, which is her whole identity."[143] Since the male penis (sex) is erased (s x), the opposition between the male genitalia (s x) and the "ideology of male dominance" (gender=culture) is an opposition in name only. As a result, Dworkin alleges that the identity of women ([s x]/gender) is constructed in opposition to the "ideology of male sexual dominance" (gender=culture).

Black Marxist feminists contend that economically privileged white feminists are not an oppressed class. For black women, the family is often a major source of succor and support; therefore, black Marxist feminists argue that reproductive controls and the institution of the family are not necessarily linked to class domination and control in patriarchal capitalism.

Angela Davis was among the first to claim that a black woman's experience of oppression challenges white feminist Marxist theory. Since black women, according to Davis, began to actively resist class oppression when they were slaves, they have traditionally displayed more power and influence than white women. Because child rearing for black women slaves was often a source of community, Davis contends that the assumption that all women are oppressed in this role by male ideology is false.

Davis also challenges the white feminist Marxist view of the relationship of women to work by pointing out that work for black women during slavery was very different from that of white women: "While a significant portion of border-state slaves may have been house servants, slaves in the Deep South—the real home of slaveocracy—were predominately agricultural workers. Around the middle of the nineteenth century, seven out of eight slaves, men and women alike, were field workers."[144]

The category race is not gender specific, and a definition of the proletariat predicated on the (s x)/gender opposition does not allow for the inclusion of race. Thus, black Marxist feminists are obliged to reconfigure the opposition. The result is an opposition between black men and women ([s x]gender)/(gender=culture) and white patriarchal capitalism ([s x]/gender)/(gender=culture) in which the linkage between biological reality (s x) and gender is erased on both sides of the equation.

The following comments by Davis illustrate how this model works: "It is a mistake to regard the institutionalized pattern of rape during slavery as an expression of white men's sexual urges. . . . Rape was a weapon of domination, a weapon of repression, whose covert goal was to extinguish slave woman's will to resist, and in the process, to demoralize men."[145] Since "white men's sexual urges" (sex) is erased (s x) in the (s x)/gender opposition between black proletariat and white patriarchal capitalism, the rape of black women becomes an act of oppression of black men as well as black women. This does not mean, of course, that Davis's argument is without merits, but it does illustrate that the (s x)/gender opposition pervades feminist theory.

While Davis includes middle-class white women in the opposition between female gender and white patriarchal oppression, other black feminists have elected not to do so. They argue that only African Americans can be black feminists, and that black men and women constitute the proletariat in opposition to the white capitalist system.[146] Once again, a (s x)/gender opposition premised on the law of the excluded middle sanctions deep and irreconcilable divisions in feminist theory.

Since a (s x)/gender opposition that links (s x) to heterosexuality does not permit the inclusion of homosexuality, lesbian Marxist feminists have also been obliged to reconfigure this opposition. The result is an opposition between homosexuality ([s x]/gender) and heterosexuality (gender=culture) which erases the linkage between sexual behavior (s x) and sexual identity. As Gloria Ansaldua observes, "The rational, the patriarchal, and the heterosexual have held sway and legal tender for too long. Third World women, lesbians, and feminist oriented men of all colors are banding and bonding together to right the balance."[147]

Because the erasure of sexual behavior erases the linkage between biological reality (sex) and sexual orientation ([s x] /gender), most lesbian Marxist feminists elect to include all women in the category lesbian. But since lesbian behavior (s x) is linked to sexual orientation in the opposition between homosexuality ([s x]/gender) and heterosexuality (gender=culture), sexual orientation can become a political issue. Hence, some lesbian Marxist feminists argue that women who allow their gender identity (s x) to be defined by heterosexual behavior (gender=culture) are collaborators with patriarchy.[148]

Adrienne Rich states that women are originally homosexual, and that women's experience, history, culture and values are separate and distinct form those of patriarchal heterosexual culture. Rich's term *compulsory heterosexuality* refers to the social power of heterosexuality which maintains its dominance with devices like romance and rape. The erasure of biological reality (s x) in the ([s x]/ gender)/ (gender=culture) opposition allows Rich to argue that heterosexuality is an arbitrary cultural construct imposed on women "globally." It also serves to legitimate the claim that "lesbian existence" and "lesbian experience" ([s x]/gender) can and should be a part of every woman's experience.

For women, writes Rich, "heterosexuality may not be a 'preference' at all but something that has to be imposed, managed, organized, propagandized, and maintained by force." She also argues that the failure to examine heterosexuality as an "institution" is "like failing to admit that the economic system called capitalism or the class system of racism is maintained by a variety of forces, including both physical violence and false consciousness."[149] Hence, lesbian existence ([s x]/gender) is "a direct or indirect attack on male right of access to women" and a "form of nay-saying to patriarchy."[150]

(S X)/GENDER AND POSTMODERNISM

Postmodern feminist theory challenges the "essentialist" view that all women construct reality in definable ways as a result of shared experiences, and attempts to move away from theoretical frameworks predicated on gender duality and asymmetry. The intent is to understand gender identity contextually or in interaction with social forces that condition this identity. In addition, there is an impulse to "go beyond gender" by "marginalizing," "decentering," or "erasing" the construct.

As philosopher Marilyn Frye observes, "What we want to do is to speak of and to and from the circumstances, experience, and perception of those who are historically, materially, and culturally constructed by or through the concept woman." The problem, says Frye, is that the concept is defined variously. "But the differences among women across cultures, locales, and generations make it clear that although all human females may live lives shaped by the same concepts of Woman, they are not all shaped by the same concept Woman."[151] Since gender duality and asymmetry arguments are predicated on the (s x)/gender opposition, postmodern feminist theory posits an opposition between variable constructions of the identity of women ([s x] /gender)/(gender=culture) and all aspects of socially constructed reality (gender=culture).

While historian Gerda Lerner recognizes that the inferior and oppressed status of women is an aspect of historical experience, she argues that the "man as oppressor" and "woman as victim" model cannot represent the contributions of women to the development of human culture: "Essentially, treating women as victims of oppression once again places them in a male-defined conceptual framework: oppressed, victimized by the standards and values of men. The true history of women is the history of their ongoing functioning in that male-defined world on their own terms." The problem, says Lerner, is that a history that focuses on the oppression excludes the story of functioning in the male-defined world: "The question of oppression does not elicit that story, and is therefore a tool of limited usefulness to the historian."[152] Given that previous feminist historians constructed women (s x)/gender in terms of a "male conceptual framework" (gender=culture), Lerner concludes that women were defined by that framework. Her solution is to construct the identity of women in terms of an opposition between ([s x]/gender)/(gender=culture) and all social constructions of reality (gender=culture). This allows the role of women in history to be constructed with much greater freedom, showing the "true history of women" to be a richly diverse "on-going functioning" in a socially constructed "male-defined world."

Although constructions of the identity of women ([s x]/gender)/(gender=culture) must be defined in opposition to social constructions of reality (gender=culture), the fact that the opposition allows the identity of women to be constructed "variously" legitimates the postmodern construct of "marginality." "Women," says Lerner, "are and always have been at least half of humankind, and most the time have been the majority. Their culturally determined and psychologically internalized marginality seems to be what makes their historical experience essentially different from that of men. But men have defined their experience as history and left women out."[153]

Because variable constructions of the identity of women ([s x]/gender)/(gender=culture) remain in opposition to socially constructed reality (gender=culture), "psychologically internalized marginality" is "culturally determined." But since the enormous range of available oppositions allows the identity of women to be constructed more independently and uniquely, women have a "marginal existence" within a male-defined social reality. In the view of most postmodern feminists, this marginal reality affords women a privileged perspective in uncovering the sources of repression in a male-dominated world.

The most radical attempts "to go beyond" the construct of gender appeal to the work of three "post-structuralist" French theorists—Michel Foucault, Jacques Lacan and Jacques Derrida. The complex history of the post-structuralist movement begins with linguist Ferdinand de Saussure's claim that the fundamental structuring principle in language is an opposition between "signifier" and "signified."

Saussure proposed that language is a system of numerous units of sounds, and a word symbol is defined within this system only in terms of acoustical differences. A word symbol is defined not by what it contains but by the system of sounds that lies outside of it; therefore, its meaning is embedded in an endless network of differences within the system. Given that the meaning of the signified cannot be defined by using more signifiers, or by words with defined and known meanings, any linguistic construction of reality refers, says Saussure, only to itself. Hence, there is no correspondence between signified (concepts in linguistically constructed reality) and signifiers (ideas composed of words with defined meanings).

Since post-structuralist theory is predicated on this signified/signifier opposition and all that it entails, Foucault, Lacan, and Derrida view human reality as a system of linguistic constructions that refers only to itself. They also maintain that there is no real or necessary connection between this reality and the world it "seems" to represent. Feminists are attracted to post-structuralist theory for several reasons. If language determines what is known, as opposed to serving as a medium through which knowledge independent of language is communicated, any aspect of male-dominated reality can be viewed as arbitrary and subjected to analysis. If all aspects of reality are arbitrary linguistic constructions, there are literally no constraints on the construction of identity in the opposition between (s x)/gender and linguistically constructed social reality (gender=culture).

Equally important, the erasure of the linkage between external, or physical, reality and linguistic constructions of this reality destroys the linkage between biological reality (sex) and linguistic constructions of this reality ([s x]/gender)/ (gender=culture). Since this allows the identity of women to be viewed as a linguistic construction with no essential or necessary referent, gender identity can be constructed "as if" the construct gender does not exist.

Foucault contends that human consciousness is created in a metaphorical "space" between word and object, or between signified and signifier, and that the evolution of personal subjectivity is a linguistic phenomenon.[154] He defines the cultural context within which human consciousness is constructed as "the total set of relations that unite, at a given period, the discursive practices that give rise to epistemological figures, sciences, and possibly formalized systems of knowledge."[155]

Since this "total set of relations," says Foucault, exists only in individual linguistic constructions of reality which refer to themselves, objective reality is unknown and unknowable. Yet, he claims, we create the illusion that the gap between subjective and objective reality can be bridged by appealing to "transcendent signifieds," or reifications such as essence, existence, truth, God, or Being. For example, Foucault would argue that since the statement, "All men are created equal" infers that human beings are "created" by "God" and attributes a universal "essence" to "men" and the abstract value "equal," this linguistic construction fosters the illusion that it represents or embodies that which lies outside itself.

Isaac D. Balbus illustrates the uses that feminists have made of Foucault's ideas: "Beneath the apparent discontinuity of transitional historical forms lies the massive continuity of male domination. It is precisely this continuity that allows us to speak of 'History' rather than 'histories.' Hence we have a situation," says Balbus, "in which gender difference is inseparable from this history: "Gender difference is either transformed into hierarchial opposition or homogenized out of existence. In neither case is that difference understood to be consistent with hierarchical egalitarian relationships between women and men. Thus it is possible to speak of History—a patriarchal history—of Western thought notwithstanding the otherwise profound differences among its various representatives."[156]

"History" is a male cultural narrative legitimated by male "transcendent signifieds" (gender=culture), and this supports the notion that there is an objective correspondence between this subjectively based narrative and external reality. But inasmuch as there is nothing outside linguistic constructions of reality in the minds of individuals ([s x]/gender) /(gender=culture), "History" is a collection of individual "histories." Hence, the task of feminist historians is to disclose how the "histories" of women ([s x] /gender)/(gender=culture) have been subsumed in "hierarchical opposition or homogenized out of existence" in a "patriarchal history" (gender=culture).

Lacan draws on Freudian theory to argue that human subjectivity, or consciousness, exists prior to linguistic constructions as "pure desire" and seeks to express itself with absolute freedom. This freedom, he claims, is constrained by "the name of the father," or the coercive power of male-defined "law." The encounter between the prelinguistic subjectivity of pure desire and the linguistically constructed "Symbolic Order" associated with the "name of the father" occurs, says Lacan, when a roughly one-year-old child looks, literally, in a mirror.

When the child sees his or her image in the mirror, there is, claims Lacan, a discrepancy between an "intuited" sense of "ideal" unity of self-sufficiency and a state of utter dependence which creates a "gap" or "rupture" between the imagined unification and its absence. But since the child must enter male defined linguistic reality, prelinguistic desire is repressed by the "Symbolic Order." The result, says Lacan, is the simultaneous emergence of linguistically based "unconscious" and "consciousness." Given that the language that constitutes the subject is imposed on the child by others, the subject is viewed as a linguistic construction that "exists" only in relation to otherness, or to the "Other." As Lacan cryptically puts it, "The subject is spoken rather than speaking."[157]

The Lacanian version of the opposition between signifier and signified takes the form of an algebraic fraction S/s where the signifier (S) is over the signified (s). The intent is to illustrate that since the signifier cannot be explained or described without resorting to an endless "chain of signifiers," "no signification can be sustained other than by reference to other signification."[158] Hence, language refers only to itself, any knowledge outside of language is unobtainable, and the space or bar in the S/s opposition is a no-thing, a nothing, a void.

Nancy Chodorow illustrates how Lacan's views have been incorporated into feminist theory: "Sexualization and subjectivity are by definition constituted in terms of difference, an opposition between the sexes that is structured linguistically and not biologically." As a result, says Chodorow,

Lacanian feminism recognizes no subjectivity apart from schematized sexual identity. Gender difference is all there is when it comes to our selfhood and subjectivity, and gender difference is experienced and cognized (through our placement in language) in terms of sexuality and gender schematization. . . . Every action is located in an unequal sexual world; we can never lose sight of our developmentally inevitable placement in a phallocentric culture.[159]

"Sexualization and subjectivity" are linguistically based constructs; therefore, the opposition between sexualization ([s x]/gender) and gender identity ([s x]/gender)/(gender=culture) is "structured linguistically and not biologically." With gender identity wholly defined by this opposition, there is "no subjectivity apart from the schematized subjectivity." Hence, human "subjectivity" (consciousness) and "action" (behavior) are defined by linguistically based phallocentric cultural narratives. The task of the feminist theory is, therefore, to disclose the identity of women ([s x]/gender)/(gender=culture) in opposition to "placement in language" (gender=culture).

Derrida argues that Western philosophy appeals to "transcendent signifieds," and that these signifieds foster the illusion that linguistic constructions of reality have "a steadfast center" of "fixed origin" which lies outside the constructions.[160] This center, he claims, is a function of a self-referential system of linguistic constructions in which each term is defined in relation to differences with other terms. Derrida coined the French neologism "differance" to suggest that the "difference" between linguistic elements designates what is "not" and contains a "trace" of what is absent.[161] The task of "deconstruction" is to uncover the "traces" by disassembling oppositions in the "systematic play of differences," and to expose what Derrida calls the "blind spot" or "aporea"—an "abyss" or void that lies at the core of all linguistic constructions of reality.

Derrida assumes that inherited texts, or cultural narratives, structure speech, and views human reality as a "text" in which rhetorical strategies and maneuvers create the illusion of unity and consistency. This "text" is a "groundless chain of signifiers," devoid of objective knowledge and universal principles. Hence, concludes Derrida, "There is nothing outside the text."[162]

The uninitiated might wonder why feminists would embrace a view of human reality that makes Nietzsche's "prison house of language" look like an upscale hotel. The answer is that deconstruction permits feminists to assume that every aspect of social, political, and economic reality can be "read" as a "text" of male domination. And it also privileges deconstruction in the analysis of these texts and deconstructionists as a class of knowers.

Consider some commentary from the deconstructionists Drucilla Cornell and Adam Thurschwell: "The deconstruction of gender categorization affirms multiplicity and the 'concrete singular,' and at the same time opens up the possibility of communicative freedom in which the Other is not there as limit but as supportive relation, the 'ground' of own being." They claim that the proper relationship between "gender categorization" and the "Other" is defined in the following statement by Derrida: "The relationship would not be asexual, far from it, but would be sexual otherwise: beyond the binary difference that governs the decorum of all codes, beyond the opposition between masculine/feminine." What, then, lies beyond binary difference? "I would like to believe," Derrida continues, "in the multiplicity of sexually marked voices. I would like to believe . . . in this mobile of nonsexual marks whose choreography can carry, divide, multiply the body of each 'individual,' whether he be classified as 'man' or 'woman' according to the criteria of usage."[163]

Since gender identity is a linguistic construction with no positive terms, the deconstruction of "gender categorization" ([s x]/gender)/(gender=culture) in opposition to the "Other" (gender=culture) is an opposition in name only. Because linguistic reality consists of "an endless chain of signifiers" in which differences in "gender categorization" are indeterminate, differences between the category "man" and the category "woman" are also indeterminate. Hence, the "binary" difference between these categories ([s x]/gender)/(gender=culture) is an illusion foisted upon us by the "decorum of codes" (gender=culture). In this way, "difference" in linguistic constructions of gender can be viewed as "a multiplicity of sexually marked voices" or a "mobile of sexual marks" ([s x]/gen-der)/(gender=culture) which cannot be reduced to gender categories in "the criteria of usage" (gender=culture).

THE FUTURE OF FEMINIST THEORY

Given the enormous investment of academic feminists in the sex/gender system, there will be an understandable tendency to deny, ignore, or rationalize away the fact that research on the sex-specific human brain has invalidated the two-domain distinction. If this is the response, the consequences could be disastrous. The problem is not merely that those outside the academy will be singularly unimpressed by a transparent attempt to defend an ideological agenda by denying the validity of scientific knowledge. It is also that second-wave feminist theory reads like a textbook example of the efficacy of scientific research on the sex-specific human brain.

It also seems clear that the erasure of biological reality allows constructions of gender identity to be defined in terms of an endless series of arbitrary and open-ended differences. Since the law of the excluded middle is foundational to these constructions, the sources of sexual inequality can be viewed as a theoretically infinite number of categorical differences. This explains why particular constituencies and interest groups have had no difficulty fashioning new theories that fit their social or political agendas, and why the history of second-wave feminist theory is marked with increasing numbers of deep divisions and conflicts.

The sex/gender system may allow women to celebrate their unbounded freedom to proliferate multiple identities in a wide range of discursive practices, but since this discourse does not recognize the relationship between bological reality and gender identity, theory, as Richard Rorty states, is sacrificed in "favor of fantasying." Because there "is no moral to these fantasies, nor any public (pedagogic or political) use to be made of them,"[164] feminist theory has become increasingly removed from political realities of the populations it intends to serve. Equally important, the now discredited notion that gender identity is entirely scripted by male cultural narratives disallows, or mitigates against, the prospect of meaningful communication and dialogue between men and women. And if I am correct about the potential sexist abuses of research on the sex-specific human brain, that dialogue will be essential as we assimilate the social and political implications of this research.

While feminists are very much aware that our current standard for sexual equality sanctions grossly unequal treatment of women, there is little or no consensus about how to revise this standard. The primary source of this confusion is the fearful prospect that recognition of essential, or biologically based, differences would eliminate barriers to sexist abuses of these differences. This accounts for the tendency in feminist scholarship to remain attached to the assumption of gender sameness as a standard for sexual equality while seeking to broaden that standard to accommodate differences that do not violate the standard. The success of this strategy has been frustrated by the sameness-difference paradox: if only things that are the same can be equal, how can we legitimate differences associated with inequalities when the standard for equality is sameness?

Although I will argue that research on the sex-specific human brain has presented us with a solution to this dilemma, it is not, of course, "the" solution. Even if we assume that the knowledge claims of science are privileged, it is absurd to suggest that they should legislate over our dealings with gender issues. Yet it appears as if our new understanding of the relationship between biological reality and gender identity can serve the goal of full sexual equality. In the next chapter, I will attempt to demonstrate that this is the case.

CHAPTER 7

The Gender Sameness Trap: Complementarity and Sexual Equality

Our society is presently in the midst of an intellectual revolution that may prove to be as significant as what Copernicus, Darwin, and Freud wrought in their fields. The earth is not the centerpiece of the solar system, human beings are not the centerpiece of creation, the ego is not the centerpiece of mind, and man is not the centerpiece of experience and knowledge— neither the generic man nor the individual man.

—CAROL TAVRIS
Mismeasure of Women

The prime-time program on ABC, narrated by John Stossel, was entitled "Boys and Girls Are Different: Men, Women and the Sex Difference."[165] Stossel first reminisced about growing up during the modern feminist movement believing that gender differences are entirely products of learning, and feminists Bella Abzug and Gloria Steinem appeared in brief sound bites to defend this position. There was no support for this view in the interviews with neuroscientists and behavioral scientists. The scientists were quite convinced that sexual differences in the human brain massively conditioned gender identity.

Although Stossel noted on several occasions that a sex-specific difference does not necessarily apply to any single individual, the logic that informed his commentary disguised this fact very nicely. It also legitimated the argument that since the brains of men and women are not the same, sex discrimination laws should be revised to reflect the differences. The Stossel program illustrates the dilemma discussed earlier. Although the two-domain distinction was intended to eliminate appeals to sexual differences in dealing with issues of sexual equality, it is predicated on the same logic we use to define sexual differences.

If the program had merely provided an account of what is known about the sex-specific human brain, it would not have aired prime time on a major commercial network. What made the program sufficiently controversial to please its corporate sponsors was the following argument: Since the brain, like the body, is sexed, gender differences are in the same class as sexual differences, and the law of the excluded middle applies to those differences. If gender differences were defined by this logic, the vast body of sex discrimination laws that protect the rights and freedoms of women would be eviscerated. This could happen in spite of the fact that our present standard of sexual equality already sanctions an enormous amount of legal abuse of women.

GENDER SAMENESS AND THE EQUALITY TRAP

A standard for sexual equality premised on the two-domain distinction and the law of the excluded middle has massively contributed to the disastrously unequal treatment of women in virtually all areas of life that specifically concern women. For example, the introduction of no-fault provisions in divorce and custody laws was widely regarded as an egalitarian triumph. Since no-fault eliminated sex-specific differences that have traditionally perpetuated the inferior status of women, the expectation was that women could now expect to be treated the same as men. But when we ignore the fact that women have children and men do not in divorce and custody hearings, some very relevant facts cease to be relevant.

Women who leave the job market to raise children typically face enormous difficulties reentering that market at competitive wages, particularly when they have dependent children. Since the vast majority of women remain the primary caretakers of dependent children, they are largely responsible for finding adequate day care, transporting children to and from dental and medical appointments, and responding to emergencies. If women in this situation are perceived as failing to compete as men, they are typically penalized with low performance evaluations, glass ceilings, meager salary increases, and loss of employment. Even those divorced women who manage to find and keep decent jobs will earn salaries that are only 70 percent of the average amount earned by men with comparable educational backgrounds and skills.

Since no-fault assumes that women already have, or can quickly achieve, the same earning power as men, the financial consequences for women have been disastrous. The standard of living for divorced women under no-fault has decreased by 73 percent, while that of a divorced men has increased by 42 percent. Women, regardless of earning power and years spent caring for children, are no longer awarded alimony in the vast majority of cases, and the average amount of child support has also declined. When women receive this support, which is less than 50 percent of the time, it represents about half the real costs of raising children. Consider two other legacies of this egalitarian triumph—90 percent of single parent households are now headed by women, and 50 percent of those households are living below the poverty line.[166]

Our current standard for sexual equality also accounts in part for our inability to curb the epidemic of domestic violence. According to Sheila James Keuhl, an attorney for the Southern California Women's Law Center, "The law has generally been interpreted from the male experience, which gives no basis for understanding how any decent, sane person would stay with an abuser. This interpretation of the law conceives of self-defense as a kind of schoolboy battle in which people of equal strength are matched, gun for gun and fist for fist."[167] In the absence of considerations of gender difference, the psychological response of women to physical abuse, death threats, and fears for the safety of children is assumed to be the same as that of men. Most courts apply the same rule of self-defense that applies to men, and refuse to recognize the pattern of dread, hopelessness, and passivity known as "battered women's syndrome."[168]

Although it is difficult to compile accurate statistics on the physical abuse of women, those we do have are very grim. According to the Department of Justice, 95 percent of spousal assaults are committed by men against women. FBI statistics show that a woman is beaten by her husband in this country every fifteen minutes, that 30 percent of the women murdered in 1990 were killed by husbands and boyfriends, and that the murderer in more than half these cases was a current or former partner.

A study done by the American Medical Association indicates that physical abuse of women by men accounts for 19 to 30 percent of the admissions of women to hospital emergency rooms, 25 percent of female suicides, and 25 percent of women seeking emergency psychiatric help. The study also estimates that 7 percent of women married to or living with a man in 1993 were physically abused by their partner, and that only 8 percent of these 3.9 million abused women revealed the source of their injuries to physicians. As Health and Human Services Secretary Donna E. Shalala states, "In this country, domestic violence is about as common as giving birth."[169]

Another legacy of the current standard for sexual equality is the manner in which judges, juries, and defense attorneys deal with female rape victims. "Sexual invasion through rape," writes legal scholar Robin West, "is understood to be a harm, and is criminalized as such, only when it involves some other harm: (such as) when it is accompanied by violence that appears in a form men understand (meaning a plausible threat of annihilation). . . . But marital rape, date rape, acquaintance rape, aggravated rape are either not criminalized, or, if they are, they are not punished."[170]

Women who press charges against a rapist typically find themselves on trial, and their appearance, demeanor, previous sexual experience, life style, social status, and their relationship, if any, to the rapist are scrutinized. In the vast majority of cases, these women are expected to defend themselves against rape and to have responded to the experience of rape as if they were men. Given this hideously unequal treatment, it is not surprising that only one in five of the estimated 26 percent of American women who become rape victims in their lifetimes report this crime.

The assumption of gender sameness also explains in part why pregnancy, PMS, and menopause are typically viewed in this culture as abnormal conditions.[171] Although there are obviously two gender-specific bodies, it is the male body that members of the medical profession are trained to view as representative or normative. Most diagrams in medical textbooks feature male bodies and depict generic bodily processes as male; descriptions of female bodily processes appear only when they do not resemble those of males. Uniquely female aspects of the human body are, therefore, made to seem deviations from the normative male body.

If a female body can be healthy only to the extent to which it resembles a healthy male body, all unique aspects of the biological life of women must be unhealthy. A "normal pregnancy" does not exist in this culture. Pregnancies are abnormal conditions made normal by the systematic application of high-tech prenatal technologies. Similarly, menstruation must be accompanied by a syndrome known as PMS, and menopause without drug therapy is quite unthinkable.

The idea that the female body is inherently diseased could also explain why a large percentage of caesareans, hysterectomies, and mastectomies performed in the United States are unwarranted.[172]

BRAIN SCIENCE
AND THE SAMENESS-DIFFERENCE PARADOX

If we wish to put an end to this legally sanctioned violence against women, perhaps there is a means to do so. The intent here is to point the way toward a more realistic and humane standard for sexual equality based on the following assumptions: (1) the scientific description of the sex- specific human brain, which includes the conditions under which this brain evolved, indicates that definitions of gender identity premised on the law of the excluded middle and the two-domain distinction are flawed; (2) the logic that is consistent with this description provides an alternative basis for defining the complex relationship between sex and gender; and (3) the resulting understanding of this relationship could legitimate an improved standard of sexual equality.

In scientific terms, the origins and character of the sex-specific human brain must be understood within the context of the evolution of our species. The genetic inheritance, or genotype, that codes differences between male and female organisms, or phenotypes, is the self-replicating molecule of life. The limpid winding staircase of human DNA consists of roughly 6 billion nucleotides in twenty-six strands, or chromosomes, which transmit information in a four-nucleotide code. The code is written in long strings of base pairs of adenine, quinine, thymine, and cytosine, and each of the estimated 100,000 human genes consists of hundreds to thousands of these base pairs. We can read this code because adenine (A) always pairs with thymine (T), and quinine (G) always pairs with cytosine (C). If, for example, one strand in a nucleotide sequence is ACGTCTCTATA, the complementary sequence is TGCAGAGATAT.

Genes code for the assemblage of proteins—three-dimensional molecules that make up the chemical and physical fabric of life. An infinite variety of proteins can be assembled by sequencing amino acids in various combinations, and this variability allows proteins to perform a staggering variety of tasks. For example, robot proteins construct tissues and organs, messenger proteins carry information throughout the body, and protein enzymes direct physiological processes.

The action of hormones on the fetal brain is variable, meaning that the activation of genes involved in sex determination is highly indeterminate; genotype is, therefore, expressed in phenotypes in "on-average" differences. Because the number of sex-specific genes are quite small in comparison with all genes involved in brain formation, shared characteristics and functions are vastly greater than differences. This explains why studies on male and female brains report findings in percentages and statistical profiles; these measures implicitly affirm that sameness is the only basis for understanding difference. The same measures are also used in studies on behavior associated with these differences. Typically, the overlap between the behavior of males and females is enormous, there is far more variation within sexes than between sexes, and a statistically significant number of females will fall well into the range of distinctly male behavior and vice versa.

THE LOGICAL FRAMEWORK
OF COMPLEMENTARITY

Obviously, the law of the excluded middle does not apply when the middle, or the genetic inheritance in the genotype and the overlap between cognitive and emotional processes in phenotypes, is the only logical basis for understanding differences. This situation requires a logic where sameness is the predicate for difference, and where profound differences between the brains and behavior of "all" men and women are narrowly defined in terms of a "general" lack of sameness. Fortunately, there is such a logic. Known as the principle of complementarity, it was developed by the Danish scientist Niels Bohr.

In an analysis of the conditions and results of observations in quantum physics, Bohr concluded that profound oppositions must be defined as follows: (1) both oppositions, when taken together, constitute a complete description of a total reality; (2) each opposition displaces the other in any observation or description of this reality; and (3) both must be kept in mind in any effort to understand the total reality.

For our purposes, the total reality of the s/he brain is contained in the genotype, and sexual differences are complementary aspects of that reality in phenotypes. Profound differences in this reality must displace one another, or fail to overlap along the entire continuum of behavioral tendencies associated with the differences and actual behavior. Differences can be understood only within the context of the total reality.

This logic expressly forbids the assumption that all characteristics of the sex-specific female brain apply to all females and vice versa. Since complementarity requires us to describe any individual human brain in terms of the total reality of the s/he brain, the enormous overlap between male and female brains is implicit in each description. The only profound gender-specific differences relevant to this description are those that utterly displace one another on the full continuum of tendencies and associated behavior.

The logic of Aristotle is predicated on difference rather than sameness, and disguises the fact that on-average differences in the sex-specific human brain are not profound. If a small percentage of males possess abstract analytical abilities that are superior on average to those of females, or a small percentage of females possess verbal skills superior on average to those of males, the law of the excluded middle entices us to conclude that all men have superior analytical abilities and all women superior verbal abilities. This is, of course, nonsense. Since both men and women fall into the superior range on each of these scales, the differences are not profound. The same applies to all human cognitive abilities.

The logic of Aristotle also explains why the assumption that only the same can be equal translates into a standard for sexual equality that perpetuates grossly unequal treatment of women. Since this logic deals in categorical oppositions between maleness and femaleness, and since equality is associated with maleness and inequality with femaleness, it follows that women should be treated the same as men. But when the standard for sexual equality is the total reality, or the entire continuum of human talent and potential, discrimination on the basis of on-average gender differences is not allowed. This standard also dictates that these differences cannot be used as the basis for defining roles or evaluating success in the performance of roles, and it does not penalize women for failing to compete as men.

The new standard would also require us to enlarge the bases for sexual equality to recognize the fact that the total reality includes sex-specific bodies and sexual responses. Paid maternity leave, adequate child care, and fair and equitable treatment of mothers in divorce and custody hearings would not be optional—they would be inalienable rights. Last, but certainly not least, the new standard would require that the punishment fit the crime in dealing with males who rape and physically abuse women.

SAMENESS, DIFFERENCE, AND COMPLEMENTARITY

What we know about this brain clearly indicates that if the law of the excluded middle is applied in assessing gender differences, the results will not be scientific. If past experience is any guide, it is also likely that this logic will be used in the service of sexist agendas. For example, when the psychologist Camilla Benbow published her paper on gender based differences in SAT scores in 1980, she made it very clear that biology was only partially responsible for the males' superior performance in mathematics. And yet network anchors and magazine and newspaper columnists proclaimed, "adolescent males are more gifted in mathematics than females." If we imagine a distribution curve that reflects this absurd conclusion, the result would look like this:

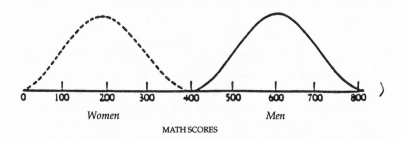

MATH SCORES

But if we look at a distribution curve that represents the overlap in the average performance of the male and female students who took this test, a very different picture emerges:

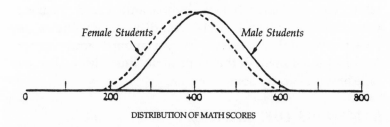

DISTRIBUTION OF MATH SCORES

Now suppose we create another graph on which the small percentage of male math prodigies is eliminated. The result would be a single bell curve indicating no discrepancies in scores. If we really intend to eliminate sexism in the response of the public to such data, however, we must also make it clear what statistical averaging means. If this had been done in 1980, the fact that female students are also math prodigies would not have been conspicuously missing in the news reports.[173]

The point is that discrepancies in cognitive abilities associated with the sex-specific neocortex are nonessential, and the logic of complementarity is the only reasonable way to assess them. This logic requires us to view sex-specific differences as complementary aspects of the total reality of the s/he brain. It also defines profound, or essential, differences as those that do not overlap along the entire continuum of human behavior. When we apply this logic to the analysis of research data on the cognitive skills of males and females, the inadequacies of usual modes of analysis become painfully apparent.

Imagine that the creators of bell curve diagrams depicting disparities in the cognitive abilities of males and females were required to produce new diagrams based on the logic of complementarity. If all of these new diagrams were superimposed on one another, the result would be a line forming a single bell curve dark at its center and fuzzy around its edges. While the fuzzy edges would indicate that the overlap was not complete, the single dark line would attest to the existence of a total reality in which gender-based cognitive differences are nonessential.

Yet nonessential differences associated with the neocortex do explain why the playing field is less than level. The fallacy that only the same can be equal obviates recognition of essential differences associated with reproductive roles and functions. It also violates the right of men and women to affirm nonessential on-average differences that they know to be real in experiential terms.

COMPLEMENTARITY
AND WOMEN'S WAYS OF KNOWING

The logic of complementarity could also be foundational to the process of revising feminist theory to reflect our new understanding of the relationship between sex and gender. Those who develop these theories should discover that the framework is a vastly more effective means of exposing the sources of sexism in cultural narratives, and can also do so in a manner that greatly enlarges the bases for meaningful dialogue between men and women. In order to illustrate how useful this logic could be, consider a text that frequently appears in women's studies courses—*Women's Ways of Knowing.*

The authors define "separate knowing" as "the game of impersonal reason," a game that has "belonged traditionally to boys."[174] Separate knowers, who tend to specialize in "masculine" disciplines ranging from philosophy to physics, are described as tough minded. "They are like doormen at exclusive clubs. They do not want to let anything in unless it is good. . . . Presented with a proposition, separate knowers immediately look for something wrong—a loophole, a factual error, a logical contradiction, the omission of contrary evidence."[175] Separate knowing is contrasted with "connected knowing," which is viewed as feminine. In place of the "doubting game," connected knowers play the "believing game." The authors allege that the "believing game" is more congenial for women because "many women find it easier to believe than doubt."[176]

Another gender theoretician, Peggy McIntosh, has developed a variant of the connected-knower versus separate-knower opposition. Why, she asks, do we study the "mountain strongholds of white men" when we need to study the "valley values" of women? The male-dominant elite, which McIntosh dubs "vertical thinkers," aims at "exact thinking, at decisiveness or mastery of something, or being able to make an argument and take on all comers, or turning in a perfect paper."[177]

Vertical thinking, writes McIntosh, is "triggered by words like excellence, accomplishment, success, and achievement." But women and, it seems, "people of color," are, she says, typically "lateral thinkers." Thinking for the laterals is more "spiritual, relational and inclusive." The aim of laterals is not to win but "to be in a decent relationship with the invisible elements of the universe."[178]

Obviously, these discrepancies in cognitive styles are consistent with the manner in which reality "tends" to be constructed in the s/he brain. But since the law of the excluded middle does not allow for the predicate of sameness, on-average differences that do not impact learning aptitude or skills are made to appear as categorical opposites. This false opposition casts women into the role of fuzzy spiritual thinkers who would rather celebrate relationships than deal with difficult subject matter. It also legitimates the absurd, not to mention insulting, conclusion that women are less competitive or skilled than men in any subject area.

THE GENDER WAR AND THE HUMAN FUTURE

When the Western world first began to come to terms with the legacy of our evolutionary past in the 1940s and 1950s, many intellectuals embraced the dark forces of biological determinism. Human beings, they proclaimed, are "animals with clothes on" victimized by inherited instincts they can neither understand nor control. Language, in the view of these harbingers of doom, was a mere overlay function, and belief in the powers of the intellect to direct and improve human experience a grand rationalization. Fortunately, advances in scientific knowledge, particularly research in neuroscience, eventually disclosed that none of these conclusions was commensurate with scientific facts.

But it strikes me as no accident that these arguments were premised on the logic of either-or. Nature abhors this logic as much as it abhors a vacuum, and it offers endless demonstrations that sameness-difference is not a paradox. Since life evolved from one source and all life forms share one parent DNA, sameness was the initial and ongoing condition of life. Similarly, the human species is a single reality, and males and females are complementary aspects of this reality.

If we want to make peace in the American gender war, there is an obvious place to start. Let us abandon the sex/gender system and work together as men and women toward an improved standard for sexual equality. Cooperation between men and women has always been critical to human survival, and the realities of men and women have always been complementary aspects of the total reality that is our symbolic universe. The difference is that the terms of survival now dictate that this cooperation must be directed toward revising the shape of this universe to reflect the total reality.

Conspicuously underrepresented on the stage of this troubled world are complementary constructions of reality associated with sex-specific differences in the female brain. The welfare of our species could well be dependent on the rapid infusion of these complementary constructions into the power elites and dominance hierarchies that shape the human future. Abandoning the sex/gender system will not be easy, and the same applies to refashioning conceptions of the gender identity based on the logical framework of complementarity. The greatest challenge, however, is not to the intellect. It is to free ourselves from the prison of the merely personal, and to enlarge our circle of compassion to embrace both complementary aspects of the total construction of reality in the s/he brain.

Notes

1. Kim Gandy, quoted in Daniel Wattenburg, "Sharia Feminist," *American Scholar*, December 1993, p. 62.

2. Kim Masters, *Vanity Fair*, November 1993, p. 170.

3. Barbara Ehrenreich, quoted in Ellis Cose, *A Man's World* (New York: HarperCollins, 1995), p. 248.

4. Margaret Mead, *Sex and Temperament in Three Primitive Societies* (New York: William Morrow, New York, 1935), p. 280.

5. Sandra Lee Bartky, *Femininity and Domination: Studies in the Phenomenology of Oppression* (New York: Routledge, 1990), p. 50.

6. Kate Millett, *Sexual Politics* (London: Virago, 1970), p. 10.

7. Virginia Held, "Feminism and Epistemology: Recent Work on the Connection Between Gender and Knowledge," *Philosophy and Public Affairs* 14, no. 3 (Summer 1989): 297.

8. David Sears, and Leone Huddy, "Women as a Political Interest Group in the Mass Public," in P. Gurin and L. Tilly, eds., *Women in Twentieth Century American Politics* (New York: Russell Sage Foundation, 1989).

9. Leone Huddy, quoted in Carol Tavris, *Anger: The Misunderstood Emotion* (New York: Simon & Schuster, 1989), p. 279.

10. Beth Schneider, "Feminist Disclaimers, Stigma, and the Contemporary Women's Movement," available from Dr. Schneider, Department of Sociology, University of California, Santa Barbara.

11. Quoted in *A Man's World*, p. 8.

12. Ibid., p. 2.

13. Judith Sherven, quoted in *A Man's World*, p. 13.

14. Quoted in *A Man's World*, p. 71.

15. See Mirra Komarovsky, *Blue-collar Marriage* (New York: Vintage, 1964).

16. Richard Driscoll, *The Binds That Tie* (Lexington, Maine: Lexington Books, 1991), p. 61.

17. Thomas A. Wills, Robert L. Weiss, and Gerald A. Patterson, "A Behavioral Analysis of the Determinants of Marital Satisfaction," *Journal of Consulting and Clinical Psychology* 42 (1974): 802-811.

18. Carol Tavris, *The Mismeasure of Women* (New York: Simon & Schuster, 1992), pp. 251-252.

19. Scott Swain, "Covert Intimacy: Closeness in Men's Friendships," in *Gender in Intimate Relationships*, B. J. Reismann, and P. Schwartz, eds. (Belmont, California: Wadsworth, 1989), p. 82.

20. Carol Tavris, *The Mismeasure of Women*, pp. 258-259.

21. Catherine K. Reismann, *Divorce Talk: Men and Women Make Sense of Personal Relationships* (New Brunswick, N.J.: Rutgers University Press, 1990), p. 153.

22. Ronald Taffel, "The Politics of Mood," *The Family Therapy Networker*, September-October 1990, p. 53.

23. Bernie Zilbergeld, *The New Male Sexuality* (New York: Bantam, 1990), p. 83.

24. Wills, Weiss, and Patterson, "A Behavioral Analysis of the Determinants of Marital Separation."

25. Survey by Yankelovith Partners, Inc., 1993.

26. See, for example, John Robertson and Louise Fitzgerald, "The(Mis)treatment of Men: Effects of Client Gender Role and Life-style on Diagnosis and Attribution of Pathology," *Journal of Counseling Psychology* 37 (1990): 3-9.

27. Tavris, *The Mismeasure of Woman*, pp. 44-45.

28. See William F. Allman, "The Mating Game," *U.S. News and World Report*, July 19, 1993, pp. 57-63.

29. Catherine A. MacKinnon, "Legal Perspectives on Sexual Difference," in Deborah L. Rhodes, ed. *Theoretical Perspectives on Sexual Difference* (New Haven, Conn.: Yale University Press, 1990), p. 216.

30. Christine Littleton, "Reconstructing Sexual Equality," *California Law Review* 75 (1987): 1282.

31. Richard Rorty, *Contingency, Irony and Solidarity* (Cambridge: Cambridge University Press, 1989), p. 125.

32. Kathleen B. Jones, *Compassionate Authority: Democracy and the Representation of Women* (New York: Routledge, 1993), p. 16.

33. J. A. H. Von Couvering, "Community Evolution and Succession in East Africa During the Last Cenozoic," A. Hill and K. Berensmeyer, eds., *Bones in the Making* (Chicago: University of Chicago Press, 1980); and R. L. Bernor, "Neogene Paleoclimatic Events and Continental Mammalian Response: Is There Global Synchroniety?" *South African Journal of Science* 81 (1985): 261.

34. T. G. Bromage, and H. B. Smith, "Dental Development in Australopithecus and Early Homo," *Nature* 232 (1985): 327.

35. See T. G. Bromage, "The Biological and Chronological Maturation of Early Hominids," *Journal of Human Evolution* 16 (1987): 257-272; and W. R. Travathan, *Human Birth: An Evolutionary Perspective* (New York: Aldine de Gruyter, 1987).

36. See Jared Diamond, *The Third Chimpanzee: The Evolution of Human Sexuality* (New York: HarperCollins, 1982), pp. 74-79.

37. A. Rosenblum, *The Natural Birth Control Book* (Philadelphia: Aquarian Research Foundation, 1976).

38. Diamond, *The Third Chimpanzee*, pp. 77-78.

39. See Helen E. Fisher, *Anatomy of Love: The Natural History of Monogamy, Adultery, and Divorce* (New York: W. W. Norton, 1992).

40. D. Symons, *The Evolution of Human Sexuality* (New York: Oxford University Press, 1979), pp. 82-83.

41. D. Rancourt-Laferriere, "Four Adaptive Aspects of the Female Orgasm," *Journal of Social and Biological Structures* 6 (1983): 319-333.

42. J. Alcock, "Ardent Adaptationism," *Natural History* (April 4, 1987); and Fisher, *Anatomy of Love*, pp. 183-184.

43. Fisher, *Anatomy of Love*, p. 184.

44. Lynn Margulis, and Dorian Sagan, *Mystery Dance: On the Evolution of Human Sexuality* (New York: Summit Books, 1991), pp. 119-120.

45. Diamond, *The Third Chimpanzee*, pp. 72-78.

46. Kathy D. Schick, and Nicholas Toth, *Human Evolution and the Dawn of Technology* (New York: Simon and Schuster, 1993).

47. J. Mehler, P. Jusczyk, G. Lambertz, N. Halsted, J. Bertoncini, and C. Amiel-Tison, "A Precursor of Language Acquisition in Young Infants," *Cognition* 29 (1988): 143-178.

48. J. F. Werker, "Becoming a Native Listener" *American Scientist* 77 (1989): 54-59.

49. Alice S. Rossi, "The Biosocial Side of Parenthood," *Human Nature* 1 (1978): 78.

50. B. Bardoni, E. Zanaria, S. Guioli, G. Floridia, K. C. Worley, G. Tonini, E. Ferrante, G. Chiumello, E. R. Mc Cabe, M. Fraccaro, et al., *Nature Genetics* 7, no. 4 (August 1994): 479-501.

51. Sondra F. Wietelson, "Neural Sexual Mosaicism: Sexual Differentiation of the Human Temporo-Parietal Region for Functional Asymmetry" *Psychoneuroendocrinology* 16, no. 1-3 (1991): 136; and L. S. Allen, R. A. Gorski, "Sexual Dimorphism of the Anterior Commissure and Massa Intermedia" *Journal of Comparative Neurology* 312, no. 1 (October 1991): 97-107.

52. M. A. Hoffman, and D. F. Swabb, "Sexual Dimorphism of the Human Brain: Myth and Reality," *Experiments in Endocrinology* 98 no. 21 (1991): 161-170; and D. F. Swabb, L. J. Gooren, and M. A. Hoffman, "Gender and Sexual Orientation in Relation to Hypothalamic Structures," *Hormone Research* 38, Supplement 2 (1992): 51-61.

53. J. C. Slimp, B. L. Hart, R. W. Goy, "Heterosexual, Autosexual and Social Behavior of Adult Male Rhesus Monkeys with Preoptic Anterior Hypothalamic Lesions," *Brain Research* 142 (1978): 105-122.

54. L. S. Allen, M. Hines, J. E. Shryne, and R. A. Gorski, "Two Sexually Dimorphic Cell Groups in the Human Brain," *Journal of Neuroscience* 9 (1988): 497-506.

55. M. A. Hoffman, and D. F. Swaab, "Sexual Dimorphism in the Human Brain: Myth and Reality," *Experimental and Clinical Endocrinology* 98, no. 2 (1991): 161-170.

56. Wietelson, "Neural Sexual Mosaicism: Sexual Differentiation of the Human Temporo-Parietal Region For Functional Asymmetry."

57. See *The Brain*, vol. 55 (Maine: Cold Spring Harbor Laboratory Press, 1990).

58. Wietelson, "Neural Sexual Mosaicism."

59. See I. Jibiki, H. Matsuda, H. Kudo, K. Kurokawa, N. Yamaguchi, and K. Hisada, "Quantitative Assessment of Regional Blood Flow with 1231-IMP in Normal Adult Subjects," *Acta-Neurol-Napoli* 15, no. 1 (1993): 7-15; and F. Okada, Y. Tokumitsu, Y. Hoshi, and M. Tamura, "Gender and Handedness-Related Differences of Forebrain Oxygenation and Hemodynamics," *Brain Research* 601, no. 1-2 (1993): 337-347.

60. See S. P. Springer, and G. Deutsch, *Left Brain, Right Brain* (San Francisco: W. H. Freedman, 1985).

61. See R. Efron, *The Decline and Fall of Hemispheric Specialization* (Hillsdale, N.J.: Erlbaum, 1990).

62. See R. G. Shulman, A. M. Blamire, D. L. Rothman, and G. McCarthy, "Nuclear Magnetic Resonance and Spectroscopy of Human Brain Function," *Proceedings of the National Academy of Sciences* 90 (April 1993): 3127-3133.

63. Bennett A. Shaywitz, Sally E. Shaywitz, Kenneth R. Pugh, R. Todd Constable, Pawel Skudlarski, Robert K. Fulbright, Richard A. Bronen, Jack M. Fletcher, Donald P. Shankweller, Leonard Katz, and John C. Gore, "Sex Differences in the Functional Organization of the Brain for Language," *Nature* 373 (February 16, 1995): 607-609.

64. Ruben C. Gur, quoted in Gina Kilota, "Man's World, Women's World? Brain Studies Point to Differences," *New York Times*, February 28,1995, p. C1.

65. Rubin C. Gur, Lyn Harper Mozley, Susan M. Resnick, Joel S. Karp, Abass Alavi, Steven E. Arnold, and Raquel E. Gur, "Sex Differences in Regional Cerebral Glucose Metabolism During a Resting State," *Science* 267, no. 5197 (January 27, 1995): 528-531.

66. See Susan U. Phillips, Susan Steele, and Christine Tanz, eds., *Language, Gender and Sex in Comparative Perspective* (Cambridge: Cambridge University Press, 1987); and David J. Martin and H. D. Hoover, "Sex Differences in Educational Achievement: A Longitudinal Study," *Journal of Early Adolescence* 7 (1987): 65-83.

67. Melissa Hines, "Gonadal Hormones and Human Cognitive Development," in Jacques Balthazart, ed., *Hormones, Brain and Behavior in Vertebrates* (Basel: Karger, 1990), pp. 51-63.

68. Jane Shibley Hyde, and Marcia C. Linn, "Gender Differences in Verbal Ability: A Meta-Analysis," *Psychological Bulletin* 104, no. 1 (1988): 53-69.

69. Doreen Kimura, "Sex Differences in the Brain," *Scientific American* (September 1992): 124-125.

70. Doreen Kimura, "Sex Differences in Cerebral Organization for Speech and Praxic Functions," *Canadian Journal of Psychology* 37, no. 1 (1983): 19-35.

71. See Robert Pool, *Eve's Rib: Searching for the Biological Roots of Sex Differences* (New York: Crown Publishers, 1994), p. 27; and Thomas Bever, "The Logical and Intrinsic Sources of Modularity," in M. Gunnar, and M. Maratos, eds., *Modularity and Constraints in*

Language and Cognition (Hillsdale, N.J.: Lawrence Erlbaum and Associates, 1992).

72. A. Mann, Sumika Sasanuma, Naoko Sakuma, and Shinobu Masaki, "Sex Differences in Cognitive Abilities: A Cross-Cultural Perspective," *Neuropsycholoaia* 28, no. 10 (1990): 1063-1077.

73. See Diane Alington, Russell Leaf, "Elimination of SAT-Verbal Sex Differences Was Due to Policy-Guided Changes in Item Content," *Psychological Reports* 68, no. 2 (1991): 541-542; and *Taking the SAT, 1992-1993* (Princeton, N.J.: Educational Testing Service, 1992).

74. See Dan R. Kenshalo, ed., *The Skin Senses* (Springfield, Ill.: Charles C. Thomas, 1968).

75. See Herbert L. Meiselman, and Robert S. Rivlin, eds., *Clinical Measurement of Taste and Smell* (New York: Macmillian Publishing Co., 1986).

76. See Marie-Olden Monneuse, France Bellisle, and Jeannine Louis Sylvestre, "Impact of Sex and Age on Sensory Evaluation of Sugar and Fat in Dairy Products," *Physiology and Behavior* 50 (1991): 1111-1117.

77. See Diane McGuinness, "Away from a Unisex Psychology: Individual Differences in Visual Perception," *Perception* 5 (1976): 279-294; and Lesle Barnes Brabyn, and Diane McGuinness, "Gender Differences in Response to Spatial Frequency and Stimulus Orientation," *Perception and Psychophysics* 26 (1979): 319-324.

78. See Colin D. Elliott, "Noise Tolerance and Extraversion in Children," *British Journal of Psychology* 62 (1971): 375-380; and Diane McGuinness, "Hearing: Individual Differences in Perceiving," 25xGsstiGn 1 (1972): 465-473.

79. B. B. Whiting, and W. H. Whiting, *Children in Six Cultures* (Cambridge, Mass.: Harvard University Press, 1975).

80. M. J. Konner, *The Tangled Wing: Biological Constraints on the Human Spirit* (New York: Harper & Row, 1982).

81. J. Money, and A. A. Ernhart, *Man and Women, Boy and Girl: The Differentiation and Dimorphism of Gender Identity From Conception to Maturity* (Baltimore, Md.: Johns Hopkins University Press, 1972).

82. See Janet Lever, "Sex Differences in the Games Children Play," Social Problems 23 (1976): 478-487; and Janet Lever, "Sex Differences in the Complexity of Children's Play and Games," *American Sociological Review* 43 (1978): 471-483; and Diane McGuinness, "Be-

havioral Tempo in Pre-School Boys and Girls," *Leaning and Individual Differences* 2, no. 3 (1990): 315-325.

83. See D. Tennov, *Love and Limerance: The Experience of Being in Love* (New York: Stein & Day, 1979).

84. H. C. Sabelli, "Rapid Treatment of Depression with Selegilinephenylalanine Combination," Letter to the Editor, *Journal of Clinical Psychiatry* 52 (1991): 3.

85. Donald G. Dutton, and Arthur P. Aron, "Some Evidence for Heightened Sexual Attraction under Conditions of High Anxiety," *Journal of Personality and Social Psychiatry* 120 (1964): 1004-1005.

86. See M. R. Liebowitz, *The Chemistry of Love* (Boston: Little, Brown,1983).

87. J. Money, *Love and Love Sickness: The Science of Sex, Gender Difference and Pair-Bonding* (Baltimore, Md.: Johns Hopkins University Press, 1980), p. 65.

88. See Liebowitz, *The Chemistry of Love*.

89. H. E. Fisher, "The Four-year Itch," *Natural History* (October 1989): 22-23.

90. Helen E. Fisher, *Anatomy of Love: The Natural History of Monogamy, Adultery, and Divorce* (New York: W. W. Norton, 1992), pp. 109-111.

91. Anastasia Toufexis, "The Right Chemicals," *Time*, February 15, 1993, p. 51.

92. Jared Diamond, *The Third Chimpanzee: The Evolution and Future of the Human Animal* (New York: HarperCollins, 1992), pp. 101-102.

93. See I. Eibil-Eibesfeldt, *Ethology: The Biology of Behavior* (New-York: Holt, Rinehart and Winston, 1970).

94. H. Hess, *The Tell-Tale Eye* (New York: Van Nostrand Reinhold, 1975).

95. See D. B. Givens, *Love Signals: How to Attract a Mate* (New York: Crown, 1983); and Fisher, *Anatomy of Love*.

96. See T. Perper, *Sex Signals: The Biology of Love* (Philadelphia: ISI Press, 1985).

97. C. S. Ford, and F. A. Beach, *Patterns of Sexual Behavior* (New York: Harper & Brothers, 1951).

98. W. R. Jankowiak, and E. F. Fisher, "A Cross-cultural Perspective on Romantic Love," *Ethnology* 31, no. 2 (1992): 149-155.

99. See S. Frayser, *Varieties of Sexual Experience: An Anthropological Perspective and Human Sexuality* (New Haven, Conn.: HRAF Press, 1985).

100. See W. H. Stephens, *The Family in Cross Cultural Perspective* (NewYork: Holt, Rinehart and Winston, 1963).

101. See P. L. van den Berghe, *Human Family Systems: An Evolutionary View* (Westport, Conn.: Greenwood Press, 1977).

102. U.S. Department of Health and Human Services, Public Health Service, "Sexual Behavior Among High School Students," 1990.

103. Ibid.

104. E. F. Furstenberg, Jr., and G. B. Spanier, *Recycling the Family: Remarriage after Divorce* (Beverly Hills, Calif.: Sage Publications, 1984).

105. R. Weis, *Marital Separation* (New York: Basic Books, 1975).

106. M. Daly, and M. Wilson, *Homicide* (New York: Aldine de Gruyter, 1988).

107. John Gagnon, Robert Michael, and Stuart Michaels, *The Social Organization of Sexuality* (Chicago: University of Chicago Press, 1994).

108. See ibid.

109. Deborah Tannen, *You Just Don't Understand: Women and Men in Conversation* (New York: Ballantine Books, 1990).

110. Ibid. p. 77.

111. Ibid., p. 51.

112. Quoted in ibid., p. 175.

113. See D. Goleman, "Two Views of Marriage Explored: His and Hers," *New York Times*, April 1, 1989.

114. See C. Gilligan, *In A Different Voice* (Cambridge: Mass.: Harvard University Press, 1982).

115. See Scott Swain, "Covert Intimacy: Closeness in Men's Friendships," in B. J. Reisman, and P. Schwartz, eds., *Gender in Intimate Relations* (Belmont, Calif.: Wadsworth, 1989).

116. See Robin T. Lakoff, *Talking Power: The Politics of Language* (New York: Basic Books, 1990).

117. See Mary Crawford, and John Gressley, "Creativity, Caring and Context: Men's and Women's Accounts of Humorous Preferences and Practices," *Psychology of Women Quarterly* 15 (1991): 217-231.

118. See Catherine K. Reissman, *Divorce Talk: Women and Men Make Sense of Personal Relationships* (New Brunswick, N.J.: Rutgers University Press, 1990).

119. Lakoff, *Talking Power*, p. 205.

120. Mary Gergen, "Life Stories: Pieces of a Dream," in G. Rosenwald, and R. Ochberg, eds., *Storied Lives* (New Haven, Conn.: Yale University Press, 1992).

121. Carol Tavris, *The Mismeasure of Women* (New York: Simon & Schuster, 1992), p. 304.

122. Thomas A. Wills, Robert L. Weiss, and Gerald R. Patterson, "A Behavioral Analysis of the Determinants of Marital Separation," in *Journal of Consulting and Clinical Psychology* 42 (1974): 802-811.

123. See John Robertson, and Louise F. Fitzgerald, "The (Mis)Treatment of Men: Effects of Client Gender Role and Life-Style on Diagnosis and Attribution of Pathology," *Journal of Counseling Psychology* 37(1990): 3-9.

124. Catherine A. MacKinnon, "Legal Perspectives on Sexual Difference," in Deborah L. Rhodes, ed. *Theoretical Perspectives on Sexual Difference* (New Haven, Conn.: Yale University Press, 1990), p. 220.

125. Deborah L. Rhodes, "Definitions of Difference," in *Theoretical Perspectives on Sexual Difference*, p. 210.

126. Sherry B. Ortner, "Is Female to Male as Nature Is to Culture?" in M. Evans, ed., *The Woman Question* (London: Fontana, 1982), p. 89.

127. Ibid., p. 92.

128. Gayle Rubin, "The Traffic in Women: Notes on the Political Economy of Sex," in M. Z. Rosaldo, and L. Lamphere, eds., *Women, Culture and Society* (Stanford, Calif.: Stanford University Press, 1974), p. 109.

129. Anne Koedt, "The Myth of the Vaginal Orgasm," in *Radical Feminism* (New York: New York Times Books, 1973), pp. 163-164.

130. Mary A. Sherfey, "A Theory of Female Sexuality," in S. Cox, ed., *Female Psychology: The Emerging Self* (Chicago: Science Research Associates, 1976), p. 184.

131. Adrienne Rich, *Of Woman Born: Motherhood as Experience and Institution* (London: Virago, 1977), p. 5.

132. Ibid., p. 166.

133. Mary Daly, *Gyn/Ecology: The Metaethics of Radical Feminism* (London: The Women's Press, 1979), p. 372.

134. Sara Riddick, "Preservative Love and Military Destruction: Some Reflections of Mothering and Peace," in J. Trebilcot, ed., *Mothering: Essays in Feminist Theory* (Riverside, N.J.: Rowan & Allenheld, 1984), p. 88.

135. Nancy Harstock, *Money, Sex and Power: Toward a Feminist Historical Materialism* (New York: Longman, 1983), p. 23.

136. Carol Gilligan, *In a Different Voice: Psychological Theory and Women's Development* (Cambridge, Mass.: Harvard University Press, 1982), p. 6.

137. Ibid., p. 168.

138. Dorothy Dinnerstein, *The Mermaid and the Minotaur* (Cambridge, Mass.: Harvard University Press, 1972), p. 66.

139. Ibid., p. 188.

140. Nancy Chodorow, *The Reproduction of Mothering: Psychoanalysis and the Sociology of Gender* (Berkeley, Calif.: University of California Press, 1978), p. 9.

141. Heidi Hartman, "Capitalism, Patriarchy, and Job Segregation by Sex," in E. Abel, and E. K. Abel, eds., *The Signs Reader: Women, Gender and Scholarship* (Chicago: University of Chicago Press, 1983).

142. Ibid., p. 88.

143. Andrea Dworkin, *Pornography: Men Possessing Women* (London: The Women's Press, 1981), p. 44.

144. Angela Davis, *Women, Race and Class* (London: The Women's Press, 1982), p. 30.

145. Ibid.

146. See G. T. Hull, et al., *All the Women Are White, All the Blacks Are Men, But Some of Us Are Brave: Black Women's Studies* (New York: The Feminist Press, 1982).

147. Gloria Ansaldua, "La Pieta," in C. Morago, and G. Ansaldua, eds., *This Bridge Called My Back: Writings by Radical Women of Color* (New York: Kitchen Table, 1983), p. 55.

148. See E. B. Freedman, et al., *The Lesbian Issue* (Chicago: University of Chicago Press, 1985).

149. Adrienne Rich, "Compulsory Heterosexuality and Lesbian Existence," in E. Abel, and E. K. Abel, eds., *The Signs Reader: Women, Gender and Scholarship* (Chicago: University of Chicago Press, 1983), p. 52.

150. Ibid., p. 62.

151. Marilyn Frye, "The Possibility of Feminist Theory," in Rhodes, ed., *Theoretical Perspectives on Sexual Difference,* p. 176.

152. Gerda Lerner, *The Majority Finds Its Past: Placing Women in History* (New York: Oxford University Press, 1979), p. 16.

153. Ibid., p. 164.

154. Michel Foucault, *The Order of Things: An Archaeology of Human Sciences* (New York: Random House, 1973), pp. 244-248.

155. Ibid., p. 71.

156. Isaac D. Balbus, "Disciplining Women," in Selya Behhabib, and Druscilla Cornell, eds., *Feminism as Critique: On the Politics of Gender* (Minneapolis: University of Minnesota Press, 1986), pp. 111-112.

157. See Jacques Lacan, *Ecrits: A Selection,* A. Sheridan, trans. (New York: W. W. Norton, 1977), pp. 19-61.

158. Ibid., p. 150.

159. Nancy J. Chodorow, "Psychoanalytic Feminism/Psychoanalytic Psychology," in Rhodes, ed., *Theoretical Perspectives on Sexual Difference,* pp. 122-123.

160. Jacques Derrida, in Richard Macksey, and Eugeneo Donato, eds., *The Structuralist Controversy* (Baltimore, Md.: Johns Hopkins University Press, 1970), pp. 247-248.

161. Jacques Derrida, *Margins of Philosophy,* A. Bass, trans. (Chicago: University of Chicago Press, 1982), pp. 3-4.

162. Jacques Derrida, *Of Grammatology,* G. C. Spivak, trans. (Baltimore, Md.: Johns Hopkins University Press, 1976).

163. Drucilla Cornell, and Adam Thurschwell, "Feminism, Negativity, and Subjectivity," in Rhodes, ed., *Feminism as Critique: On the Gender of Politics,* pp. 161-162.

164. Richard Rorty, *Contingency Irony and Solidarity* (Cambridge: Cambridge University Press, 1989), p. 125.

165. ABC, 9:00 P.M. EST, February 2, 1995.

166. See Mary Ann Mason, *The Equality Trap* (New York: Simon & Schuster, 1988); and Carol Tavris, *The Mismeasure of Women* (New York: Simon & Schuster, 1992).

167. Sheila James Keuhl, "Understanding the Battered Reality," op-ed article, *Los Angeles Times,* January 7, 1990.

168. Tavris, *The Mismeasure of Women,* p. 112.

169. Don Coburn, "Domestic Violence," *Washington Post Health Magazine,* June 28, 1994, p. 10.

170. Robin West, "Jurisprudence and Gender," *The University of Chicago Law Review* 55 (1988): 59.

171. See Tavris, *The Mismeasure of Women*.

172. Lynda Burke, and Sandy Best, "The Tyrannical Womb: Menstruation and Menopause," in *Alice Through the Microscope: The Power of Science over Women's Lives* (London: Virago, 1980).

173. See Robert Sapolsky, "The Case of the Falling Nightwatchmen," *Discover*, July 1987, pp. 42-45.

174. Mary Field Belenky, Blythe Mcvicker Clinchy, Nancy Rule Goldberg, and Jill Mattick Tarule, *Women's Ways of Knowing* (New York: Basic Books, 1986), p. 104.

175. Ibid.

176. Ibid., p. 113.

177. Peggy McIntosh, "Seeing Our Way Clear: Feminist Revision and the Academy," *Proceedings of the Eighth Annual GLCA Women's Studies Conference* (Ann Arbor, Mich.: Great Lakes Colleges Association, November 5-7, 1982), p. 13.

Bibliography

Ackerman, C. 1963. Affiliations: Structural Determinants of Differential Divorce Rates. *American Journal of Sociology* 69: 13-20.

Ackerman, D. 1990. *The Natural History of the Senses.* New York: Random House.

Ackerman, S. 1989. European History Gets Even Older. *Science* 246: 28-29.

Adams, V. 1991. Getting at the Heart of Jealous Love. *Psychology Today* (May): 38-48.

Alcock, J. 1987. Ardent Adaptationisms. *Natural History,* April 4.

Alexander, R. D. 1974. The Evolution of Social Behavior. *Annual Review of Ecology and Systematics* 5: 325-383.

Alexander, R. D. 1987. *The Biology of Moral Systems.* New York: Aldine de Gruyter.

Alexander, R. D., and K. M. Noonan. 1979. Concealment of Ovulation, Parental Care and Human Social Evolution. In N. A. Chagnon and W. Irons, eds. *Evolutionary Biology and Human Social Behavior,* North Scituate, Mass.: Duxbury Press.

Alington, Diane, and Russell Leaf. 1991. Elimination of SAT-Verbal Sex Differences Was Due to Policy-Guided Changes in Item Content. *Psychological Reports* 68, no. 2: 541-542.

Allen, L. S., and R. A. Gorski. 1991. Sexual Dimorphism of the Anterior Commissure and Massa Intermedia. *Journal of Comparative Neurology* 312, no. 1 (October): 97-107.

Allen, L. S., M. Hines, J. E. Shryne, and R. A. Gorski. 1988. Two Sexually Dimorphic Cell Groups in the Human Brain. *Journal of Neuroscience* 9: 497-506.

Allman, William F. 1993, July 19. The Mating Game. *U.S. News and World Report* (July 19): 57-63.

Ansaldua, Gloria. 1983. La Pieta. In C. Morago, and G. Ansaldua, eds. *This Bridge Called My Back: Writings by Radical Women of Color*. New York: Kitchen Table.

Atwater, L. 1987. College Students' Extramarital Involvement. *Sexuality Today* (November 30): 2.

Balbus, Isaac D. 1987. Disciplining Women. In Selya Benhabib, and Drucilla Cornell, eds. *Feminism as Critique: On the Politics of Gender*. Minneapolis: University of Minnesota Press.

Bardoni, B., E. Zanaria, S. Guioli, G. Floridia, K. C. Worley, G. Tonini, E. Ferrante, G. Chiumello, E. R. McCabe, M. Fraccara, et al. 1994, August. *Nature Genetics* 7, no. 4 (August): 479-501.

Barnes, J. 1967. The Frequency of Divorce. In A. Epstein, ed. *The Craft of Social Anthropology*. London: Tavistock.

Bartky, Sandra Lee. 1990. *Femininity and Domination: Studies in the Phenomenology of Oppression*. New York: Routledge.

Belenky, Mary Field, et al. 1986. *Women's Ways of Knowing*. New York: Basic Books.

Belkin, L. 1989. Bars to Equality of Sexes Seen as Eroding, Slowly. *New York Times*, August 20.

Bell, A. P., and S. Weinberg. 1978. *Homosexualities: A Study of Diversity among Men and Women*. New York: Simon and Schuster.

Bell, D. 1980. Desert Politics: Choices in the Marriage Market. In Mona Etienne, and Eleanor Leacock, eds. *Women and Colonization*. New York: Praeger.

Benbow, C. P. 1983. Sex Differences in Mathematical Reasoning Ability: More Facts. *Science* 222: 1029-1031.

Benbow, C. P., and J. C. Stanley. 1980. Sex Differences in Mathematical Ability: Fact or Artifact. *Science* 210: 1234-1236.

Benderly, B. L. 1987. *The Myth of Two Minds: What Gender Means and Doesn't Mean.* New York: Doubleday.

Benshoof, L., and R. Thornill. 1987. The Evolution of Monogamy and Concealed Ovulation in Humans. *Journal of Social and Biological Structures* 2: 95-106.

Bernard J. 1964. The Adjustment of Married Mates. In H. I. Christensen, ed. *Handbook of Marriage and the Family.* Chicago: Rand McNally.

Bernor, R. L. 1985. Neogene Paleoclimatic Events and Continental Mammalian Response: Is There Global Synchroniety? *South African Journal of Science* 81: 261.

Betzig, L. L. 1982. Despotism and Differential Reproduction: A Cross Cultural Correlation of Conflict Asymmetry, Hierarchy and Degree of Polygamy. *Ethology and Sociology* 3: 209-221.

Betzig, L. L. 1986. *Despotism and Differential Reproduction: A Darwinian View of History.* Hawthorne, New York: Aldine.

Betzig, L. L. 1989. Causes of Conjugal Dissolution: A Cross-Cultural Study. *Current Anthropology* 30: 654-76.

Bever, Thomas. 1992. The Logical and Intrinsic Sources of Modularity. In M. Gunnar, and M. Maratos, eds. *Modularity and Constraints in Language and Cognition.* Hillsdale, N.J.: Lawrence Erlbaum.

Binford, L. R. 1981. *Bones: Ancient Men and Modern Myths.* New York: Academic Press.

Binford, L. R. 1985. Human Ancestors: Changing View of Their Behavior. *Journal of Anthropological Archaeology* 4:292-327.

Binford, L. R. 1987. The Hunting Hypothesis: Archaeological Methods and the Past. *Yearbook of Physical Anthropology* 30: 1-9.

Blumenschine, R. J. 1986. *Early Hominid Scavenging Opportunities: Implications for Carcass Availability in the Serengeti and Ngorongoro Ecosystems.* British Archaeological Reports International Series, no. 283. Oxford: BAR.

Blumenschine, R. J. 1987. Characteristics of Early Hominid Scavenging Niche. *Current Anthropology* 28: 383-407.

Borgerhoff Mulder, M. 1990. Kipsigis Women's Preferences for Wealthy Men: Evidence for Female Choice in Mammals? *Behavioral Ecology and Sociobiology* 27: 255-264.

Botwin, B. 1988. *Men Who Can't Be Faithful.* New York: Warner Books.

Brabyn, Lesle Barnes, and Diane McGuinness. 1979. Gender Differences in Response to Spatial Frequency and Stimulus Orientation. *Perception and Psychophysics* 26: 319-324.

Brain, C. K. 1981. *The Hunters or the Hunted? An Introduction to African Cave Taphonomy.* Chicago: University of Chicago Press.

Bromage, T. G. 1987. The Biological and Chronological Maturation of Early Hominids. *Journal of Human Evolution* 16: 257-272.

Bromage, T. G., and H. B. Smith. 1986. Dental Development in Australopithecus and Early Homo. *Nature* 232: 327.

Bullough, V. L. 1976. *Sexual Variance in Society and History.* Chicago: University of Chicago Press.

Burke, Lynda, and Sandy Best. 1980. The Tyrannical Womb: Menstruation and Menopause. In *Alice through the Microscope: The Power of Science over Women's Lives.* London: Virago.

Burley, N. 1979. The Evolution of Concealed Ovulation. *American Naturalist* 114: 835-858.

Buss, D M. 1989. Sex Differences in Human Mate Preference: Evolutionary Hypothesis Tested in 37 Cultures. *Behavioral and Brain Sciences* 12: 1-49.

Cant, J.G.H. 1981. Hypothesis for the Evolution of Human Breasts and Buttocks. *American Naturalist* 117: 199-204.

Chance, N. A. 1966. Social Behavior and Primate Evolution. In M.F.A. Montagu, ed. *Culture and the Evolution of Man.* New York: Oxford University Press.

Chodorow, Nancy J. 1978. *The Reproduction of Mothering: Psychoanalysis and the Sociology of Gender.* Berkeley: University of California Press.

Chodorow, Nancy J. 1990. Psychoanalytic Feminism/Psychoanalytic Psychology. In Deborah L. Rhodes, ed. *Theoretical Perspectives on Sexual Difference.* New Haven, Conn.: Yale University Press.

Clark, G. 1980. *Mesolithic Prelude.* Edinburgh: Edinburgh University Press.

Coburn, Don. 1994. Domestic Violence. *Washington Post Health Magazine,* June 28, p. 10.

Cohen. M. N. 1977. *The Food Crisis in Prehistory: Overpopulation and the Origins of Agriculture.* New Haven, Conn.: Yale University Press.

Cohen, Y. A. 1964. *The Transition from Childhood to Adolescence: Cross Cultural Studies in Initiation Ceremonies, Legal Systems and Incest Taboos.* Chicago: Aldine.

Cose, Ellis. 1995. *A Man's World.* New York: HarperCollins.

Crawford, Mary, and John Gressley. 1991. Creativity, Caring and Context: Men's and Women's Accounts of Humorous Preferences and Practices. *Psychology of Women Quarterly* 15: 217-231.

Daly, M. 1978. The Cost of Mating. *American Naturalist* 112: 771-774.

Daly, M. 1983. *Sex, Evolution and Behavior: Adaptations for Reproduction.* North Scituate, Mass.: Duxbury Press.

Daly, M., and M. Wilson. 1988. *Homicide.* New York: Aldine de Gruyter.

Daly, Mary. 1979. *Gyn/Ecology: The Metaethics of Radical Feminism.* London: The Women's Press.

Daniels, D. The Evolution of Concealed Ovulation and Self-Deception. *Ethology and Sociobiology* 4: 69-87.

Davis, Angela. 1982. *Women, Race and Class.* London: The Women's Press.

Deaux, Kay, and Branda Major. 1990. A Social-Psychological Model of Gender. In Deborah L. Rhodes, ed., *Theoretical Perspectives on Sexual Difference.* New Haven, Conn.: Yale University Press.

Degler, C. N. 1991. *In Search of Human Nature: The Decline and Revival of Darwinianism in American Social Thought.* New York: Oxford University Press.

Delson, E., ed. 1985. *Ancestors: The Hard Evidence*. New York: Alan R. Liss.

Derrida, Jacques. 1970. In Richard Macksey, and Eugeneo Donato, eds. *The Structuralist Controversy*. Baltimore, Md: Johns Hopkins University Press.

Derrida, Jacques. 1976. *Of Grammatology*. Trans. G. C. Spivak. Baltimore, Md.: Johns Hopkins University Press.

Derrida, Jacques. 1982. *Margins of Philosophy*. Trans. A. Bass. Chicago: University of Chicago Press.

Diamond, Jared. 1982. *The Third Chimpanzee: The Evolution of Human Sexuality*. New York: HarperCollins.

Driscoll, Richard. 1991. *The Binds That Tie*. Lexington, Mass.: Lexington Books.

Dutton, Donald G., and Arthur P. Aron. 1964. Some Evidence for Heightened Sexual Attraction under Conditions of High Anxiety. *Journal of Personality and Social Psychiatry* 120: 1004-1005.

Dworkin, Andrea. 1981. *Pornography: Men Possessing Women*. London: The Women's Press.

Efron, R. 1990. *The Decline and Fall of Hemispheric Specialization*. Hillsdale, N.J.: Erlbaum.

Eibil-Eibesfeldt, I. 1970. *Ethology: The Biology of Behavior*. New York: Holt, Rinehart and Winston.

Elliott, Colin D. 1971. Noise Tolerance and Extraversion in Children. *British Journal of Psychology* 62: 375-380.

Emlen, S. T., and L. W. Oring. 1977. Ecology, Sexual Selection and the Evolution of Mating Systems. *Science* 197: 215-223.

Epstein, C. 1988. *Deceptive Distinctions: Sex, Gender and the Social Order*. New York: Russell Sage.

Fedigan, L. M. 1982. *Primate Paradigms: Sex Roles and Social Bonds*. Montreal: Eden Press.

Feinman, S., and G. W. Gill. 1978. Sex Differences in Physical Attractiveness Preferences. *Journal of Social Psychology* 105: 43-52.

Fennema, E., and G. C. Leder, eds. 1990. *Mathematics and Gender*. New York: Teachers College Press.

Fisher, H. E. 1982. *The Sex Contract: The Evolution of Human Behavior*. New York: William Morrow.

Fisher, H. E. 1987. Evolution of Human Serial Pairbonding. *American Journal of Physical Anthropology* 78: 331-54.

Fisher, H. E. 1989r. The Four-year Itch. *Natural History* (October): 22-23.

Fisher, Helen E. 1992. *Anatomy of Love: The Natural History of Monogamy, Adultery, and Divorce.* New York: W. W. Norton.

Ford, C. S., and F. A. Beach. 1951. *Patterns of Sexual Behavior.* New York: Harper and Brothers.

Foucault, M. 1973. *The Order of Things: An Archaeology of Human Sciences.* New York: Random House.

Foucault, M. 1985. *The History of Sexuality,* Vol. 2, Trans. R. Hurley. New York: Pantheon Books.

Frank, R. 1985. *Choosing the Right Pond: Human Behavior and the Quest for Status.* New York: Oxford University Press.

Frayser, S. 1985. *Varieties of Sexual Experience: An Anthropological Perspective* and *Human Sexuality.* New Haven, Conn.: HRAF Press.

Freedman, E. B., et al. 1985. *The Lesbian Issue.* Chicago: University of Chicago Press.

Frye, Marilyn. 1990. The Possibility of Feminist Theory. In Deborah L. Rhodes, ed. *Theoretical Perspectives on Sexual Difference.* New Haven, Conn.: Yale University Press.

Furstenberg, F. F., Jr., and G. B. Spanier. 1984. *Recycling the Family: Remarriage after Divorce.* Beverly Hills, Calif.: Sage Publications.

Gagnon, John, Robert Michael, and Stuart Michaels. 1994. *The Social Organization of Sexuality.* Chicago: University of Chicago Press.

Gallup, G. G. 1982. Permanent Breast Enlargement in Human Females: A Sociological Perspective. *Journal of Human Evolution* 11: 597-601.

Gerfersen, E. 1982. *Sexual Practices: The Story of Human Sexuality.* London: Mitchell Beazley.

Gergen, Mary. 1992. Life Stories: Pieces of a Dream. In G. Rosenwald, and R. Ochberg, eds. *Storied Lives.* New Haven, Conn.: Yale University Press.

Gilligan, C. 1982. *In a Different Voice: Psychological Theory and Women's Development*. Cambridge, Mass.: Harvard University Press.

Givens, D. B. 1989. *Love Signals: How to Attract a Mate*. New York: Crown.

Goldin, C. 1990. *Understanding the Gender Gap: An Economic History of Men and Women*. New York: Oxford University Press.

Goleman, D. 1989. Two Views of Marriage Explored: His and Hers. *New York Times*, April 1.

Goleman, D. 1989. Subtle But Intriguing Differences Found in the Brain Anatomy of Men and Women. *New York Times*, April 11.

Gould, J. L., and C. G. Gould. 1989. *The Ecology of Attraction: Sexual Selection*. New York: W. H. Freeman.

Gur, Rubin C., Lyn Harper Mozley, Susan M. Resnick, Joel S. Karp, Abass Alavi, Steven E. Arnold, and Raquel E. Gur. 1995. Sex Differences in Regional Cerebral Glucose Metabolism During a Resting State. *Science* 267, no. 5197 (January 27): 528-531.

Hall, R. L. 1982. *Sexual Dimorphism in Homo Sapiens: A Question of Size*. New York: Praeger.

Harstock, Nancy. 1983. *Money, Sex and Power: Toward a Feminist Historical Materialism*. New York: Longman.

Hartman, Heidi. 1983. Capitalism, Patriarchy, and Job Segregation by Sex. In E. Abel, and E. K. Abel, eds. *The Signs Reader: Women, Gender and Scholarship*. Chicago: University of Chicago Press.

Held, Virginia. 1989. Feminism and Epistemology: Recent Work on the Connection Between Gender and Knowledge. *Philosophy and Public Affairs* 14, no. 3 (summer): 111-149.

Hess, E. H. 1975. *The Tell-Tale Eye*. New York: Van Nostrand Reinhold.

Hines, Melissa. 1990. Gonadal Hormones and Human Cognitive Development. *Hormones, Brain and Behavior in Vertebrates*, edited by Jacques Balthazard, pp. 51-53. Basel: Karger.

Hoffman, M. A., and D. F. Swaab. 1991. Sexual Dimorphism in the Human Brain: Myth and Reality. *Experimental and Clinical Endocrinology* 98, no. 2: 161-170.

Hopson, J. L. 1979. *Scent Signals: The Silent Language of Sex.* New York: William Morrow.

Hull, G. T., et al. 1982. *All the Women Are White, All the Blacks Are Men, But Some of Us Are Brave: Black Women's Studies.* New York: The Feminist Press.

Hyde, Jane Shibley, and Marcia C. Linn. 1988. Gender Differences in Verbal Ability: A Meta-Analysis. *Psychological Bulletin* 104, no. 1: 53-69.

Jankowiak, W. R., and E. F. Fisher. 1992. A Cross-cultural Perspective on Romantic Love. *Ethnology* 31, no. 2: 149-155.

Jibiki, I., H. Matsuda, H. Kudo, K. Kurokawa, N. Yamaguchi, and K. Hisada. 1993. Quantitative Assessment of Regional Blood Flow with 1231-IMP in Normal Adult Subjects. *Acta-Neurol-Napoli* 15, no. 1: 7-15.

Jones, Kathleen B. 1993. *Compassionate Authority: Democracy and the Representation of Women.* New York: Routledge.

Kenshalo, Dan R., ed. 1968. *The Skin Senses.* Springfield, Ill.: Charles C. Thomas.

Keuhl, Sheila James. 1990. Understanding the Battered Reality. *Los Angeles Times*, January 7.

Kilota, Gina. 1995. Man's World, Women's World? Brain Studies Point to Differences. *New York Times*, Februrary 28, p. C1.

Kimura, Doreen. 1983. Sex Differences in Cerebral Organization for Speech and Praxic Functions. *Canadian Journal of Psychology* 37: 19-35.

Kimura, Doreen. 1992. Sex Differences in the Brain. *Scientific American* (September): 124-125.

Koedt, Anne. 1973. The Myth of the Vaginal Orgasm. In *Radical Feminism.* New York: New York Times Books.

Komarovsky, Mirra. 1964. *Blue-collar Marriage.* New York: Vintage.

Konner, M. J. 1982. *The Tangled Wing: Biological Constraints on the Human Spirit.* New York: Harper and Row.

Konner, M. J. 1988. Is Orgasm Essential? *Sciences* (March-April): 4-7.

Lacan, Jacques. 1977. *Ecrits: A Selection*. Trans. A. Sheridan. New York: W. W. Norton.

Laitman, J. T. 1984. The Anatomy of Human Speech. *Natural History* (August): 20-27.

Lakoff, Robin T. 1990. *Talking Power: The Politics of Language*. New York: Basic Books.

Lawrence, R. J. 1989. *The Poisoning of Eros: Sexual Values in Conflict*. New York: Augustine Moore Press.

Leder, G. C. 1990. Gender Differences in Mathematics: An Overview. In *Mathematics and Gender*. edited by E. Fennema, and G. C. Leder. New York: Teachers College Press.

Lerner, Gerda. 1979. *The Majority Finds Its Past: Placing Women in History*. New York: Oxford University Press.

Lever, Janet. 1976. Sex Differences in the Games Children Play. *Social Problems* 23: 478-487.

Lever, Janet. 1978. Sex Differences in the Complexity of Children's Play and Games. *American Sociological Review* 43: 471-483.

Lewin, R. 1982. How Did Humans Evolve Big Brains? *Science* 216: 840-841.

Lieberman, P. 1984. *The Biology and Evolution of Language*. Cambridge, Mass.: Harvard University Press.

Littleton, Christine. 1987. Reconstructing Sexual Equality. *California Law Review* 75: 1282.

MacKinnon, Catherine A. 1990. Legal Perspectives on Sexual Difference. In Deborah L. Rhodes, ed. *Theoretical Perspectives on Sexual Difference*. New Haven, Conn.: Yale University Press.

Mann, A., Sumiko Sasanuma, Naoko Sakuma, and Shinobu Masaki. 1990. Sex Differences in Cognitive Abilities: A Cross-Cultural Perspective. *Neuropsychologia* 28, no. 10: 1063-1077.

Mansperger, M. C. 1990. The Precultural Human Mating System. *Journal of Human Evolution* 5: 245-259.

Margulis, Lynn, and Dorian Sagan. 1991. *Mystery Dance: On the Evolution of Human Sexuality.* New York: Summit Books.

Martin, David J., and H. D. Hoover. 1987. Sex Differences in Educational Achievement: A Longitudinal Study. *Journal of Early Adolescence* 7: 65-83.

Mascia-Lees, F. E., J. H. Relethford, and T. Sorger. 1986. Evolutionary Perspectives on Permanent Breast Enlargement in Human Females. *American Anthropologist* 88: 423-29.

Mason, Mary Ann. 1988. *The Equality Trap.* New York: Simon and Schuster.

Masters, Kim. 1993. The Lorena Bobbitt Case. *Vanity Fair,* November.

McGuiness, D. 1976. Perceptual and Cognitive Differences Between the Sexes. In B. Lloyd, and J. Archer, eds. *Explorations in Sex Differences.* New York: Academic Press.

McGuiness, D. 1985. Sensory Biases in Cognitive Development. In R. L. Hall, P. Draper, M. E. Hamilton, D. McGuiness, C. M. Otten and E. A. Roth, eds. *Male-Female Differences: A Bio-Cultural Perspective.* New York: Praeger.

McGuinness, Diane. 1972. Hearing: Individual Differences in Perceiving. *Perception* 1: 465-473.

McGuinness, Diane. 1976. Away from a Unisex Psychology: Individual Differences in Visual Perception. *Perception* 5: 279-294.

McGuinness, Diane. 1990. Behavioral Tempo in Pre-School Boys and Girls. *Learning and Individual Differences* 2, no. 3: 315-325.

McIntosh, Peggy. 1982. Seeing Our Way Clear: Feminist Revision and the Academy. In *Proceedings of the Eighth Annual GLCA Women's Studies Conference,* November 5-7. Ann Arbor, Mich.: Great Lakes Colleges Association.

Mead, Margaret. 1935. *Sex and Temperament in Three Primitive Societies.* New York: William Morrow.

Mehler, J., P. Jusczyk, G. Lambertz, N. Halsted, J. Bertoncini, and C. Amiel-Tison. 1988. A Precursor of Language Acquisition in Young Infants. *Cognition* 29: 143-178.

Meiselman, Herbert L., and Richard S. Rivlin, eds. 1986. *Clinical Measurement of Taste and Smell.* New York: Macmillan.

Mellen, S.L.W. 1981. *The Evolution of Love.* San Francisco: W. H. Freeman.

Michod, R. E., and B. R. Leven, eds. 1987. *The Evolution of Sex: An Examination of Current Ideas.* Sunderland, Mass.: Sinauer.

Millett, Kate. 1970. *Sexual Politics.* London: Virago.

Money, J. 1980. *Love and Love Sickness: The Science of Sex, Gender Difference and Pair-Bonding.* Baltimore. Md.: Johns Hopkins University Press.

Money, J., and A. A. Ernhart. 1972. *Man and Women, Boy and Girl: The Differentiation and Dimorphism of Gender Identity from Conception to Maturity.* Baltimore, Md.: Johns Hopkins University Press.

Monneuse, Marie-Olden, France Bellisle, and Jeannine Louis-Sylvestre. 1991. Impact of Sex and Age on Sensory Evaluation of Sugar and Fat in Dairy Products. *Physiology and Behavior* 50: 1111-1117.

Okada, F., Y. Tokumitsu, Y. Hoshi, and M. Tamura. 1993. Gender and Handedness-Related Differences of Forebrain Oxygenation and Hemodynamics. *Brain Research* 601, no. 1-2: 337-347.

Ortner, Sherry B. 1982. Is Female to Male as Nature Is to Culture? In M. Evans, ed. *The Woman Question.* London: Fontana.

Peck, J. R., and M. W. Feldman. 1988. Kin Selection and the Evolution of Monogamy. *Science* 240: 1672-1674.

Perper, T. 1985. *Sex Signals: The Biology of Love.* Philadelphia: ISI Press.

Phillips, Susan U., Susan Steele, and Christine Tanz, eds. 1987. *Language, Gender and Sex in Comparative Perspective.* Cambridge: Cambridge University Press.

Pool, Robert. 1994. *Eve's Rib: Searching for the Biological Roots of Sex Differences.* New York: Crown Publishers.

Price, D., and J. A. Brown, eds. 1985. *Prehistoric Hunter-Gatherers: The Emergence of Cultural Complexity.* New York: Academic Press.

Rancourt-Laferriere, D. 1983. Four Adaptive Aspects of the Female Orgasm. *Journal of Social and Biological Structures* 6: 319-333.

Reismann, Catherine K. 1990. *Divorce Talk: Men and Women Make Sense of Personal Relationships.* New Brunswick, N.J.: Rutgers University Press.

Rhodes, Deborah L. 1990. Definitions of Difference. In Deborah L. Rhodes, ed. *Theoretical Perspectives on Sexual Difference.* New Haven, Conn.: Yale University Press.

Rich, Adrienne. 1977. *Of Woman Born: Motherhood as Experience and Institution.* London: Virago.

Rich, Adrienne. 1983. Compulsory Heterosexuality and Lesbian Existence. In E. Abel, and E. K. Abel, eds. *The Signs Reader: Women, Gender and Scholarship.* Chicago: University of Chicago Press.

Riddick, Sara. 1984. Preservative Love and Military Destruction: Some Reflections of Mothering and Peace. In J. Trebilcot, ed. *Mothering: Essays in Feminist Theory.* New Jersey: Rowan and Allenheld.

Robertson, John, and Louise F. Fitzgerald. 1990. The (Mis)treatment of Men: Effects of Client Gender Role and Life-style on Diagnosis and Attribution of Pathology. *Journal of Counseling Psychology* 37: 3-9.

Rorty, Richard. 1989. *Contingency, Irony and Solidarity.* Cambridge: Cambridge University Press.

Rosenblum, A. 1976. *The Natural Birth Control Book.* Philadelphia: Aquarian Research Foundation.

Rossi, Alice S. 1978. The Biosocial Side of Parenthood. *Human Nature* 1: 78.

Rubin, Gayle. 1974. The Traffic in Women: Notes on the Political Economy of Sex. In M. Z. Rosaldo, and L. Lamphere, eds. *Women, Culture and Society.* Stanford, Calif.: Stanford University Press.

Sabelli, H. C. 1991. Rapid Treatment of Depression with Selegiline-phenylalanine Combination. Letter to the Editor. *Journal of Clinical Psychiatry* 52: 3.

Sacks, K. 1979. *Sisters and Wives: The Past and Future of Sexual Equality.* Urbana: University of Illinois Press.

Sapolsky, Robert. 1987. The Case of the Falling Nightwatchmen. *Discover* (July): 42-45.

Schick, Kathy D., and Nicholas Toth. 1993. *Human Evolution and the Dawn of Technology.* New York: Simon and Schuster.

Schneider, Beth. 1995. Feminist Disclaimers, Stigma, and the Contemporary Women's Movement. Available from Dr. Schneider, Department of Sociology, University of California, Santa Barbara.

Sears, David, and Leone Huddy. 1989. Women as a Political Interest Group in the Mass Public. In P. Gurin, and L. Tilly, eds. *Women in Twentieth Century American Politics.* New York: Russell Sage Foundation.

Shaywitz, Bernett A., Sally E. Shaywitz, Kenneth Pugh, R. Constable, Todd Skudlarski, M. Pawel, Robert K. Fulbright, Richard A. Bronen, Jack M Fletcher, Donald P. Shankweller, Leonard Katz, and John C. Gore. 1995. Sex Differences in the Functional Organization of the Brain for Language. *Nature* 373 (February 16): 607-609.

Sherfey, Mary. 1976. A Theory of Female Sexuality. In S. Cox, ed. *Female Psychology: The Emerging Self.* Chicago: Science Research Associates.

Sherman, M. J. 1972. *Sex-Related Cognitive Differences: An Essay on Theory and Evidence.* Springfield, Ill.: Charles C. Thomas.

Shulman, R. G., A. M. Blamire, D. L. Rothman, and G. McCarthy. 1993. Nuclear Magnetic Resonance and Spectroscopy of Human Brain Function. *Proceedings of the National Academy of Sciences* vol. 90: 3127-3133.

Simons, E. L. 1985. Origins and Characteristics of the First Hominids. In E. Delson, ed. *Ancestors: The Hard Evidence.* New York: Alan R. Liss.

Sommers, Christina Hoff. 1994. *Who Stole Feminism? How Women Have Betrayed Women.* New York: Simon and Schuster.

Springer, S. P., and G. Deutsch. 1985. *Left Brain, Right Brain.* San Francisco: W. H. Freedman.

Stephens, W. N. 1963. *The Family in Cross Cultural Perspective.* New York: Holt, Rinehart and Winston.

Swabb, D. F., L. J. Gooren, and M. A. Hoffman. 1989. Gender and Sexual Orientation in Relation to Hypothalamic Structures. *Hormone Research* 38, Supplement 2: 51-61.

Swain, Scott. 1989. Covert Intimacy: Closeness in Men's Friendships. In B. J. Reisman, and P. Schwartz, eds. *Gender in Intimate Relations.* Belmont, Calif.: Wadsworth.

Symons, D. 1979. *The Evolution of Human Sexuality.* New York: Oxford University Press.

Tannen, Deborah. 1990. *You Just Don't Understand: Women and Men in Conversation.* New York: Ballantine Books.

Tavris, Carol. 1989. *Anger: The Misunderstood Emotion.* New York: Simon and Schuster.

Tavris, Carol. 1992. *The Mismeasure of Women.* New York: Simon and Schuster.

Tennov, D. 1979. *Love and Limerance: The Experience of Being in Love.* New York: Stein and Day.

Tiger, L. 1992. *The Pursuit of Pleasure.* Boston: Little, Brown.

Toufexis, Anastasia. 1993. The Right Chemicals. *Time* (February 15): 51.

Travathan, W. R. 1987. *Human Birth: An Evolutionary Perspective* New York: Aldine de Gruyter.

Turke, P. W. 1984. Effects of Ovulatory Concealment and Synchrony on Protohominid Mating Systems and Parental Roles. *Ethology and Sociobiology* 5: 33-44.

U.S. Department of Health and Human Services. 1990. Public Health Service, Sexual Behavior among High School Students.

van der Berghe, P. L. 1977. *Human Family Systems: An Evolutionary View.* Westport, Conn.: Greenwood Press.

Von Couvering, J.A.H. 1980. Community Evolution and Succession in East Africa During the Last Cenozoic. In A. Hill, and K. Berensmeyer, eds. *Bones in the Making.* Chicago: University of Chicago Press.

Wattenburg, Daniel. 1993, December. Sharia Feminist. *American Scholar:* 62.

Weis, R. 1975. *Marital Separation.* New York: Basic Books.

Werker, J. F. 1989. Becoming a Native Listener. *American Scientist* 77: 54-59.

bibliography

West, Robin. 1988. Jurisprudence and Gender. *University of Chicago Law Review* 55: 59.

Whiting, B. B., and W. M. Whiting. 1975. *Children in Six Cultures.* Cambridge, Mass.: Harvard University Press.

Whyte, M. K. *Dating, Mating and Marriage.* New York: Aldine de Gruyter.

Wietelson, S. F. 1991. Neural Sexual Mosaicism: Sexual Differentiation of the Human Temporo-Parietal Region For Functional Asymmetry. *Psychoneuroendocrinology* 16, no. 1-3: 131-155.

Williams, G. C. 1975. *Sex and Evolution.* Princeton, N.J.: Princeton University Press.

Wills, Thomas A., Robert L. Weiss, and Gerald R. Patterson. 1974. A Behavioral Analysis of the Determinants of Marital Separation. *Journal of Consulting and Clinical Psychology* 42: 802-811.

Zihlman, A. L. 1981. Women as Shapers of the Human Adaptation. In F. Dahlberg, ed. *Woman the Gatherer.* New Haven, Conn.: Yale University Press.

Zilbergeld, Bernie. 1990. *The New Male Sexuality.* New York: Bantam.

Index

About the Author

ROBERT L. NADEAU, a professor in the Department of English and Environmental Science at George Mason University, works to bridge the gap between the culture of the humanities and the culture of the sciences. His research and writing explore the societal impacts of advances in science and technology.